# BUILDING HAPPINESS, RESILIENCE AND MOTIVATION IN ADOLESCENTS

*of related interest*

**What Children Need to be Happy, Confident and Successful**
**Step by Step Positive Psychology to Help Children Flourish**
*Jeni Hooper*
ISBN 978 1 84905 239 9
eISBN 978 0 85700 483 3

**Working with Children and Teenagers Using Solution Focused Approaches**
**Enabling Children to Overcome Challenges and Achieve their Potential**
*Judith Milner and Jackie Bateman*
ISBN 978 1 84905 082 1
eISBN 978 0 85700 261 7

**A Short Introduction to Promoting Resilience in Children**
*Colby Pearce*
ISBN 978 1 84905 118 7
eISBN 978 0 85700 231 0
*JKP Short Introductions series*

**Helping Adolescents and Adults to Build Self-Esteem**
**A Photocopiable Resource Book**
*Deborah M. Plummer*
ISBN 978 1 84310 185 7
eISBN 978 1 84642 051 1

**The Big Book of Therapeutic Activity Ideas for Children and Teens**
**Inspiring Arts-Based Activities and Character Education Curricula**
*Lindsey Joiner*
ISBN 978 1 84905 865 0
eISBN 978 0 85700 447 5

**Cool Connections with Cognitive Behavioural Therapy**
**Encouraging Self-esteem, Resilience and Well-being in Children and Young People Using CBT Approaches**
*Laurie Seiler*
ISBN 978 1 84310 618 0
eISBN 978 1 84642 765 7

**Communication Skills for Working with Children and Young People**
**Introducing Social Pedagogy**
**3rd edition**
*Pat Petrie*
ISBN 978 1 84905 137 8
eISBN 978 0 85700 331 7

# BUILDING HAPPINESS, RESILIENCE AND MOTIVATION IN ADOLESCENTS

Ruth MacConville and Tina Rae

A POSITIVE PSYCHOLOGY CURRICULUM FOR WELL-BEING

Jessica Kingsley *Publishers*
London and Philadelphia

First published in 2012
by Jessica Kingsley Publishers
116 Pentonville Road
London N1 9JB, UK
and
400 Market Street, Suite 400
Philadelphia, PA 19106, USA

*www.jkp.com*

**Library of Congress Cataloging in Publication Data**
MacConville, Ruth.
  Building happiness, resilience and motivation in adolescents : a positive psychology curriculum for well-being / Ruth MacConville and Tina Rae.
     p. cm.
  Includes bibliographical references.
  ISBN 978-1-84905-261-0 (alk. paper)
  1. Positive psychology. 2. Happiness in adolescence. 3. Resilience (Personality trait) in adolescence. 4. Motivation (Psychology) in adolescence. I. Rae, Tina. II. Title.
  BF204.6.M33 2012
  155.5'19--dc23
                      2011048663

**British Library Cataloguing in Publication Data**
A CIP catalogue record for this book is available from the British Library

ISBN 978 1 84905 261 0
eISBN 978 0 85700 548 9

Printed and bound in Great Britain

# CONTENTS

## Part 1 Facilitating the Programme

# Part II Delivering the Programme

# FACILITATING THE PROGRAMME

# INTRODUCTION

Welcome to our book. For those readers who want to find out immediately about delivering the programme which forms its backbone, it might be best to turn to Part II of this resource. For those readers who want to know more about the theory behind the programme and the context of the book, read on.

Positive psychology, properly understood and applied, offers insight for every individual within the school. This book translates the key findings of this new science into a resource that will enable schools to build a 'strengths approach' based on this new science. Its aim is to provide a practical resource for practitioners who want an overview of the research and a rich and varied repertoire of activities distilled into a stand-alone curriculum that they can deliver in their own classrooms.

The importance of individuals knowing and using their strengths is central to positive psychology because they relate to understanding and building each individual's psychological health and well-being. Greater well-being in turn enhances learning, the traditional goal of education. Martin Seligman (2011), the architect of positive psychology, explains that this is because positive mood produces broader attention, more creative thinking and more holistic thinking whereas negative mood produces narrowed attention and critical and analytical thinking.

Although both positive and negative thinking are important in the right situation, Seligman suggests that schools all too often emphasise critical thinking and following orders rather than creative thinking and learning new stuff, and this frequently leads to disenchantment with learning and disengagement with school. He writes '…in the modern world I believe that we have arrived at an era in which more creative thinking, less rote following of orders and yes, even more enjoyment – will succeed better' (Seligman 2011, p.80).

## A strengths approach

Ilona Boniwell (2006), founder of the European Network of Positive Psychology, explains that a 'strengths approach' challenges two basic assumptions about human nature. First, that everyone can learn to be competent in almost anything; and second, that the greatest potential for growth is in the areas of the person's greatest weakness. Positive psychologists suggest that top achievers know their capabilities, set their goals slightly above their current level of performance and therefore achieve them. In contrast, low achievers are unaware of their abilities and frequently set unrealistically high goals that they fail to achieve. Top achievers build their lives on their talents and strengths and set out to manage their weaknesses rather than develop them.

The purpose of this resource is to enable students to recognise their strengths and talents, develop them and create new ways of using them in their daily lives. Research on the value of strengths suggests that knowing and following one's strengths:

- encourages insight and perspective in one's life

- generates optimism

- provides a sense of direction

- helps to develop confidence

- generates a sense of vitality

- brings a sense of fulfilment

- helps achieve one's goals.

The development of certain strengths also helps build resilience and provides a buffer against depression and other mental health issues.

It is increasingly recognised that schools have a vital role to play in promoting emotional health and well-being and enable children and young people to develop their capabilities and flourish. Recent decades have seen big increases in the proportion of young people with social, emotional and behavioural difficulties. Mental health issues are increasingly prevalent in young people and these difficulties affect all areas of a young person's life and increase the likelihood of mental health difficulties later on in adult life. Seligman writes:

> the prevalence of depression among young people is shockingly high worldwide. By some estimates depression is about ten times more common than it was fifty years ago… it now ravages teenagers: fifty years ago, the average age of first onset was about thirty… all of us in the field are dismayed by how much depression there is now and how most of it goes untreated. (Seligman 2011, p.79)

This book is designed to be a practical and informed starting point which will enable practitioners to develop a strengths-based approach to building resilience, happiness and motivation in young people.

## Using this book

This book is written in parts and sections that interlock like a jigsaw. Following this opening, there is an introduction to the theory of positive psychology that underpins the programme.

Section 2 of Part I of the book contains a PowerPoint presentation that can be used to introduce the programme to staff. Then Section 3 provides guidance notes for facilitators on delivering the programme.

Part II contains the 24 chapters on character strengths that form the programme, clustered under six virtues.

## About the programme

The programme presented in this book introduces the core elements of positive psychology and conveys these concepts in a clear and practical way. It offers a creative and engaging way of teaching young people the attitude change, knowledge, practice and skill development that are essential for their well-being. This approach is consistent with the school's role in developing young people's cognitive and social skills. Throughout the programme students are introduced to the key insights of positive psychology. These include:

- developing flexible thinking skills
- learned optimism
- understanding and developing signature strengths
- holding a growth mindset.

The programme aims to teach students the practical skills that they can use to make their lives go better. The sessions are necessarily interactive and are largely based on group discussion and partner work to ensure that the students learn more about themselves and others. The sessions are intended to be delivered with a sense of fun and celebration to ensure that all students are engaged and inspired.

Students are encouraged to practise the skills and ideas that are introduced in the sessions in their everyday lives so that they are able to initiate for themselves positive changes in their lives. Samuel Smiles (quoted in Ben-Shahar 2007), father of the modern, self-help movement, wrote that, 'Every youth should be made to feel that his happiness and wellbeing in life must necessarily rely mainly on himself and the exercise of his own energies, rather than upon the help and patronage of others.'

This book does not claim to be an exhaustive account of positive psychology. Rather, it is designed to provide a practical and informed starting point for practitioners who recognise the importance of facilitating well-being in schools and settings through an explicit 'stand-alone' curriculum.

Our vision in writing this book is that positive psychology and a 'strengths' approach should become a resource for all practitioners because it has the capacity to focus our beliefs and practice on the positives – what works well – provide a solution to the increasing epidemic of depression amongst young people and provide a way of enabling young people to engage with their strengths and talents.

## Positive psychology

### What is positive psychology?

Positive psychology was officially launched as a field of study in 1998 by Martin Seligman when he became president of the American Psychological Society. Seligman (2006) defines this new science as 'an umbrella term for the study of positive emotions, positive character traits and enabling institutions.' An important goal for positive psychology is advancing knowledge about how to help people increase their level of happiness, positive mental health and personal thriving. It brings scientific tools to the study of what makes individuals flourish and the conditions that create flourishing lives. Its focus is not just on individuals but also on families, organisations and cultures. Ilona Boniwell (2006) in her excellent introduction to this emerging science, *Positive Psychology in a Nutshell*, explains that it operates on three different levels:

- the subjective level
- the individual level
- the group level.

The subjective level is about feeling good, rather than doing good or being a good person. It includes the study of positive experiences such as joy, well-being, satisfaction, contentment, happiness and flow.

The second level is about the individual and the aim is to identify the constituents of the 'good life' and the personal qualities that are necessary for being a 'good person', through studying human strengths and virtues, future mindedness, capacity for love, courage, perseverance, forgiveness, originality, wisdom, interpersonal skills and giftedness.

Finally, at the group or community level, the emphasis is on civic virtues, social responsibilities, nurturance, altruism, civility, tolerance, work ethics, positive institutions and other factors that contribute to the development of citizenship and community.

This resource will mainly concentrate on the second level. However, it will inevitably also touch on the first and third level as the three levels are interlinked.

Positive psychology has arisen as an antidote to psychology's traditional emphasis on what is not working: depression, mental illness, disorders, failings and weaknesses. Buckingham and Clifton write:

> …guided by the belief that good is the opposite of bad, mankind has for centuries pursued its fixation with fault and failing. Doctors have studied disease in order to learn about health. Psychologists have investigated sadness in order to learn about joy. Therapists have looked into the causes of divorce in order to learn about happy marriage and in schools and workplaces around the world, each one of us has been encouraged to identify, analyse and correct our weaknesses in order to be strong. (Buckingham and Clifton 2005, p.2)

Martin Seligman sums this position up when he writes, 'I have spent most of my life working on psychology's venerable goal of relieving misery and uprooting the disabling conditions of life' (Seligman 2011, p.1).

Seligman and Csikszentmihalyi (2000, p.8) explain that positive psychology's focus is to 'reorient psychology back to its two neglected missions – making normal people stronger and more productive and making high human potential actual.' According to positive psychologists, traditional psychology or 'psychology as usual' has been concerned with the negative aspects of human life: depression, mental illness, disorders, failings and weaknesses; and psychological interventions have previously focused on reducing weakness, suffering and anxiety rather than on increasing happiness and well-being. The assumption underlying these practices appears to be that if a person's suffering can be relieved, well-being will be the outcome for that individual. If, for example, individuals are victims of their childhood experiences it was believed that they could only recover if they relive and understand their past.

Dan Nettle (2005) suggests, however, that research into post-traumatic stress and critical incident debriefing, which has become the norm in contemporary society, has shown that counselling after such events can make individuals worse not better. Evidence from neuroscience suggests that by talking about bad events we stop them fading away through 'extinction' and simply keep reactivating the experience. This is because people have a natural healing mechanism which makes them resilient and our minds are designed like our bodies, to repair themselves. Counselling or psychological interventions can get in the way of spontaneous healing and for many individuals excessive refocusing on their past has had a reinforcing or 'framing' effect, making it more difficult for them to progress.

When left unexamined, Dan Nettle suggests that bad memories do not fester like an untreated wound. Rather they tend to fade away through extinction. Brain research over the past few years has demonstrated that talking about old and painful memories keeps them alive. This idea is not new.

## Strengths have their own patterns

Felicia Huppert (2007) believes that the study of well-being has been neglected partly because it was assumed that if we understood the causes of stress, anxiety, depression and the variety of negative emotions then the absence of these human adversities would result in human flourishing. For example, if poverty caused unhappiness then wealth would cause happiness; if poor physical health caused unhappiness then good physical health would cause happiness. Faults and failings deserve study, but they do not tell us much about strengths. Strengths have their own patterns. However, it is clear that wealth is only weakly linked to happiness; people in good health are often miserable while those with poor health may be happy. Evidence has been accumulating to show that the absence of illness is not a sufficient criterion for health.

Huppert and her fellow researchers at Cambridge University have highlighted the fact that the causes of happiness are not necessarily the opposite of the causes of unhappiness; strengths have their own patterns and flourishing is much more than the absence of misery. Positive psychologists have emphasised that the causes and consequences of human flourishing should be studied in their own right.

Positive psychology is psychology adopting the same scientific methods. However, it studies different topics and asks different questions, such as 'What works?' rather than 'What doesn't work?' This new movement is about rebalancing our interests to highlight the fact that we also need to study the positives, what is right as well as what is wrong. It has been evolving and expanding over the past decade and it now has a vast literature as a flood of books have been published on happiness and well-being. They include lifestyle books, self-help books and scientific volumes. Researchers and positive psychologists have earned section status within the American Psychological Association's (APA) Division 17 (Society of Counselling Psychology) and have also generated enough research to merit a comprehensive *Handbook of Positive Psychology* (Snyder and Lopez 2002). All of these publications confirm what science has demonstrated, that given a certain level of economic well-being, happiness – or flourishing as Martin Seligman (2011) now prefers to call it – comes not from money or from owning cool possessions but from successful personal relationships and engagement in meaningful activities, both of which depend upon understanding and developing our signature (higher) character strengths.

Positive psychologists do not claim to have invented the good life or to have introduced its scientific study; however, standing on the shoulders of giants such as Aristotle and Marcus Aurelius and building on the pioneering work of Maslow (1971), Erikson (1963), Valliant (1977) and many others they have enhanced our understanding of how, why and when positive emotions, positive character and the institutions that facilitate them flourish. The value of the new science lies in its work of uniting a disparate body of research about what makes life worth living.

The study of happiness, despite its robust scientific and psychological credentials, has nevertheless had a bad press and has been characterised by pop psychology offering fun and charisma yet seldom much substance. Tal Ben-Shahar (2007) explains that the teaching of happiness is often associated with a lack of rigour and symbolised by a plethora of smiley faces. There continues to be a widespread view that happiness is at best a soft option and at worst part of the culture of entitlement which seeks instant success, increases self-obsession and undermines resilience. Martin Seligman has recently suggested that one of the problems with 'happiness' is that it 'underexplains' what we choose and the modern ear immediately hears 'happy' to mean buoyant mood, merriment, good cheer and smiling. He writes:

> I actually detest the word happiness which is so overused that it has become almost meaningless. It is an unworkable term for science or for any practical goal such as education, therapy, public policy or just changing your personal life. (Seligman 2011, p.9)

Seligman now believes that the topic of positive psychology is well-being and the 'gold standard' for measuring well-being is flourishing. Well-being according to Seligman has five measurable elements that count towards it. They are:

1. positive emotion (of which happiness and life satisfaction are elements)
2. engagement
3. relationships
4. meaning
5. achievement.

According to Seligman's revised theory of positive psychology, happiness which was previously its centrepiece is now only part of the wider construct of well-being. The goal of well-being is to increase the amount of flourishing in one's life and on the planet. To flourish an individual must have all of three 'core features':

1. positive emotions
2. engagement and interest
3. meaning and purpose.

An individual must also have three of six 'additional features':

1. self-esteem

2. optimism

3. resilience

4. vitality

5. self-determination

6. positive relationships.

Historically, however, happiness was not simply tied to pleasure. The idea that the inner life is what matters most if we are to flourish came from the Greeks, and the notion that happiness is based on virtues or qualities is the main theme of the ethics of the Greek Rationalist, Aristotle. More than two thousand years ago Aristotle set out his belief that we are created for happiness and it is the ultimate goal (Barnes 1984). No-one, argued Aristotle, ever seeks happiness as a means to something else. With the sole exception of happiness, everything we humans desire can be regarded as a means to some higher end, and that higher end is usually happiness.

## *Three ascending levels of happiness*

More recently Dan Nettle (2005) has described three ascending levels of happiness which incorporate the historical view of happiness as being about ideals and wanting something greater, deeper, vaster than ourselves, something that outstrips our selfish desires and personal goals.

- *Level 1:* The most immediate and direct state of happiness involves an emotion or feelings like joy or pleasure. The feeling comes about because a desired state is attained. There is not much cognition involved beyond the recognition that the desired thing has happened.

- *Level 2:* When people say they are happy with their lives they usually don't mean that they are experiencing pleasure in their lives all the time. Rather they mean that on reflection, on the balance sheet of pleasure and pain, the balance is reasonably positive over the long term. Level 2 happiness is not so much concerned with pleasure and feelings as with judgements about the balance of feelings and can be summed up by terms such as contentment and life satisfaction.

- *Level 3:* This state cannot be easily measured as it involves a broader sense of happiness and can be summed up by Aristotle's ideal of the good life termed 'eudaimonia' which refers to a life in which the person flourishes and fulfils his/her true potential.

Needless to say, throughout this resource we are using the term happiness to describe a state that is over and above positive emotion: pleasure, warmth, comfort. Rather, we are using it in the sense of Dan Nettle's higher levels of happiness and as such it is about engagement and meaning and therefore the term is interchangeable with Seligman's (2011) 'well-being' and 'flourishing'.

## What really makes us happy?

Seligman (2011) writes that the goal of positive psychology in well-being theory is to measure and to build human flourishing. Achieving this goal starts by asking what really makes us happy. Studies by Sonja Lyubomirsky (2007) suggest that each individual appears to have a set point or characteristic level of happiness which is genetically determined and accounts for 50 per cent of each individual's happiness quota. According to this theory we all inevitably return to our individual set point following disruptive life events. This means that winning the lottery, getting married or divorced, being involved in a traumatic accident may increase or decrease our set point of happiness temporarily; however, within a few months we will return to our individual set point.

## Adaptation

The process by which we return to our characteristic happiness level after experiencing either positive or negative events is known as 'adaptation'. We come equipped with what behavioural scientist Daniel Gilbert (2007) calls a 'psychological immune system' that makes us expect bad things to be worse than they generally turn out to be. Because we imagine that our reactions to bad events will never fade, our own powers of recuperation take us by surprise. We also adjust to positive events more rapidly than we anticipate. We acclimatise and get used to the good and the bad things that happen to us.

## Circumstances

The most counterintuitive finding in Lyubomirsky's (2007) study is that only 10 per cent of the variance in our happiness levels is explained by differences in life circumstances or situations, that is, whether we are rich or poor, married or divorced. This means that if all individuals had the same set of circumstances (same house, partner, looks, bank balance) the difference in happiness levels would only be reduced or increased by 10 per cent.

## Intentional activities

After taking into account our genetic background and our circumstances, the third factor is our behaviour – the intentional and effortful practices in which each individual engages. Lyubomirsky suggests that the key to changing our happiness lies not in changing our genetic make up (even if we could) or in changing our circumstances – for example, by becoming wealthier or more successful – but in our daily intentional activities which account for 40 per cent of our happiness potential. For each individual there is a significant 40 per cent of room to manoeuvre, for opportunities to increase or decrease our happiness levels, through what we do in our daily lives.

This of course is good news and means that we are all in effect the architects of our own happiness. Over the past decade positive psychologists have begun to construct cautious answers to the question, 'What makes us happy?' We now know, based on verifiable evidence, that there are plenty of things we can do to make ourselves and others happier. Becoming happier, however, is not an easy option; it takes knowledge, commitment and hard work because it is about enabling individuals to realise their highest levels of human potential.

## The importance of daily, intentional activities for happiness

Lessons from positive psychology suggest that flourishing – that is, achieving a level of happiness and well-being that is over and above pleasure – is the consequence of personal effort and something that has to be fought for. The concept of striving for happiness dates from the time of the Roman Empire. Marcus Aurelius (Staniforth 1964) who ruled the Roman Empire from AD 161 to 180, recorded his thoughts in a private document that he entitled 'To Myself'. Marcus Aurelius believed that the process of becoming happier is more like wrestling than dancing because it requires us to stand prepared and unshaken and deal with what comes along and those things that we did not foresee. The message from down the ages is that you have to keep working at happiness – you don't just arrive at a blissful destination and stay there for the rest of your life. Over and over again the match must be re-fought and the victory gained anew.

Aristotle also believed that just as one swallow does not make a summer, one pleasant day does not make a whole life happy. Flourishing is therefore an activity, requiring skill, concentration, focus and active effort. Dan Nettle (2005) uses the analogy of athleticism to illustrate the fact that well-being, like fitness, is a matter of degree – just as with fitness you would not expect to go straight from gloom to joy, but with effort you can become progressively more able to cope with adversity and become calmer and more joyful. Some individuals are naturally more athletic than others; however, everybody can increase his or her level of athleticism by training. Training is effortful, however, and individuals vary in their response to it; when it is not kept up individuals return to their original baseline. The quality of one's life can be gradually transformed not because of any change in one's external circumstances, but because one's inner life gradually becomes stronger. Increasing our happiness then depends on daily intentional activities. Intentional activities may be:

- cognitive; regularly adopting an optimistic or positive attitude
- behavioural; regularly being kind and thoughtful to others, engaging in exercise
- inspirational; identifying and working towards meaningful, personal goals.

## Money, that's what I want

The idea of improving our individual level of happiness through engaging in intentional activities which require effort on a daily basis is fairly alien in our society. Traditionally when individuals are asked what would improve the quality of life their most common answer has been 'more money'. The illusion, promoted by advertisers through a constant stream of psychologically sophisticated messages, is that the route to happiness is through consumerism – spending money on products. Clever propaganda seeks to exploit our personal vulnerabilities in order to sell us more stuff. Children and young people are included in this drive towards consumerism and are particularly susceptible to messages tying security, self-worth, love and friendship to the purchase of cool possessions. The widespread fascination with celebrities and the increasing level of distress experienced by many young people are continually reported in the media.

James (2007) writes that, in his experience, many young people seem to be fixated upon being famous, regardless of whether they have talent or are prepared to work hard. James quotes a conversation overheard between two nine-year-old girls who were asked what they wanted to be when they were older:

'Famous,' said one.

'Famous for what?'

'Er, I don't know, being an actress or a TV presenter, something like that.'

James suggests that preoccupation with being a celebrity is widespread amongst young people and cites a survey of English children reported in *The Observer* by Anushka Asthana (2004). Asked to name 'the best things in the world', children put 'being famous' at the top of their lists followed by family, football and holidays.

In her book *Toxic Childhood*, Sue Palmer (2006) reports that the developed world, especially the most economically successful countries including USA, Japan and the UK, is suffering an epidemic of misery among its young and suggests, on the basis of an ongoing World Health Organisation study 'Young People's Health in Context', that by 2020 psychiatric disorders in children and young people will increase by 50 per cent compared with other health issues, making them one of the five main causes of disability and death.

## How to flourish

Central to the field of positive psychology is the paradox that the human brain has a negative default position. This negativity bias of the brain means that it is very easy for individuals to be fearful, isolated and pessimistic and we therefore have to learn how to keep our negativity in check by increasing our experience of positive emotions. Dan Nettle (2005) suggests that in order to flourish we need to:

- reduce the impact of negative emotions
- increase positive emotions
- change the subject – that is, think about other people rather than ourselves.

## Reduce the impact of negative emotions

Overall, negative emotions have been shown to narrow our outlook. They warn us about a specific threat and when we feel fear it is almost always preceded by a thought of danger. When we feel sad there is always a thought of loss. When we feel angry, there is always a thought of injustice. This moment of thought leaves us a brief space and room to pause– that is, to think about what is really going on and intervene so that our negative emotional reaction is not out of proportion to the reality of danger, loss or injustice.

Albert Ellis (1962) created the ABC (adversity, belief, consequence) model to help us understand and control our reactions to adversity. Ellis observed that rather than the adversity itself it is our belief about the cause of adversity that actually triggers our feeling response and behaviour – that is, adversity leads to belief which leads to consequences. It is not what happens to us that causes our reactions, rather it is what we think about what has happened that determines our response. A key strategy from positive psychologists is for individuals to learn to reframe their responses– that is, to identify negative thoughts and replace them with realistic alternatives. Neuroscientists tell us that the more frequently that optimistic thoughts are rehearsed the more natural they become. With practice, reframing and consciously generating optimistic thoughts can become an automatic response. Learned optimism is about thinking accurately about real problems and taking the time to consider issues in a realistic and non-negative way.

## Learned optimism

In the 1960s Martin Seligman was involved in research into what is termed 'learned helplessness'. Individuals with this mindset have learnt that they have no control over a situation, expect to fail now and anticipate this to be true in the future. Therefore they give up. Seligman recognised the need to give people the psychological defences to deal with the feelings of helplessness that can lead to depression and recognised that it was possible to teach people how to be optimistic and thus develop resilience through building control and mastery over their lives.

## Explanatory style

Seligman *et al.*'s (1995) approach to building optimism is cognitive, that is, equipping individuals with a new way of thinking about the world. It is described in their book *The Optimistic Child* which contains a programme designed to promote optimism in school-aged children at risk of depression. They explain:

> …the basis of optimism does not lie in positive phrases or images of victory, but in the way you think about causes. Each of us have habits of thinking about causes, a personality trait I call 'explanatory style'. Explanatory style divides into two types: pessimistic and optimistic. It develops in childhood, and without explicit, direct intervention is lifelong. (Seligman *et al.* 1995, p.52)

## The three 'P's

Seligman *et al.* describe the three dimensions of explanatory style which individuals use to explain why any particular good or bad event happens. The three dimensions are:

1. *Permanence*: this addresses whether a person believes that the cause of a bad event is permanent, that is, never changing (the pessimistic view), or temporary (the optimistic view).

2. *Pervasiveness*: this is concerned with the individual's belief about the extent of the problem, whether it is global and affects everything (the pessimistic view) or specific and affects only one thing (the optimistic view).

3. *Personalisation*: this addresses a person's view of whose fault it is that a negative event occurred.

Seligman *et al.* use the term 'general self-blame' to describe the pessimist's view that it is a 'generalised personal flaw' that is the cause of the problem. The optimist's view is called 'behavioural self-blame' as the optimist puts the blame down to a particular 'one-off' behaviour or action, not a personality characteristic or flaw. A student with a pessimistic explanatory style who receives poor exam results might conclude that the result was an outcome of being stupid. An optimistic student in the same situation would be more likely to conclude that the poor result was an outcome of not studying hard enough.

## Restructuring one's thinking

In their book *The Optimistic Child* Seligman *et al.* (1995) suggest that the key to developing an optimistic outlook is to restructure one's thinking. This involves learning four key skills:

1. The first skill involves recognising the negative thoughts that flit through one's mind when one is feeling low. These thoughts can be pervasive and undermine one's mood.

2. The second skill involves evaluating these thoughts. This means recognising that the things you say to yourself may not be true.

3. The third skill is the ability to generate more accurate explanations.

4. The fourth skill is 'decatastrophising' or stopping yourself planning for the worst because doing this can be a drain on your energy and ruin your mood.

## Think good, feel good

The next stage in developing an optimistic mindset is to build the link between thinking and feeling, emphasising that how we feel does not just come out of the blue. Although it is tempting to believe that feeling bad is triggered by stress or by challenge or any negative event that happens to us, that link, emphasise Seligman *et al.*, is not as straightforward as it may appear. This idea is certainly not new. The ability to reframe negative events by searching for a perspective that is both truthful and favourable enables individuals to maintain a realistically optimistic perspective.

## Resilience

Resilience is closely related to optimism. It is a cognitive skill that enables us to climb over life's obstacles rather than be defeated by them. Resilient individuals believe that the world is a changeable place over which they can exert influence and transform the world from being a hostile, frightening place to a place of opportunity. The term 'resilience' has typically been used to describe individuals who have overcome great stress and hardship. Early research in the area of resilience suggested that there was something remarkable about young people who overcame great adversity and studies focused on individual characteristics, such as temperament, intelligence, problem solving and stress resistance. In later studies the focus on individual characteristics changed to include an emphasis on the importance of the protective factors in the environment that reduce the impact of the risk factors. These protective factors include:

- the importance of family and a secure base

- education

- friendships and positive peer relationships.

It is now recognised that building resilience involves a two-pronged approach:

- building personal coping skills
- developing protective factors in the individual's environment.

The personal coping skills (adapted from Brown 2010) which enable a young person to be resilient include:

- being resourceful and having effective coping skills

- a willingness to ask for help

- the self-knowledge that they can do something that will enable them to manage their feelings and cope

- trust in the social support that is available to them

- strong connection to family and friends.

Resilience theory has been influenced and strengthened by positive psychology and psychologists now take the view that all aspects of life are there to be embraced and, in fact, coping with risk and challenge are good for us. Resilience theory therefore has relevance for all children and young people. The protective factors that enable individuals to 'bounce back' from adversity also enable individuals to bounce forward to face new challenges and achieve their goals. The demands of growing up in today's society mean that we all need to deal with life's challenges and difficulties. Stress and adversity are now an inevitable part of life for us all. Carol Craig, chief executive of the Centre for Confidence and Wellbeing in Glasgow, writes, 'even with the best care, for children and young people the world can be full of adversity' (Craig 2007, p.92). For some this is positive as struggles, hardship and challenges are considered to be necessary components of an emotionally rich life. Adversity isn't always to be avoided therefore; it is a necessary prerequisite to building resilience.

## Increase positive emotions

The 'Broaden-and-Build' theory of positive emotions developed by Barbara Fredrickson (2009), the winner of the first Templeton prize in positive psychology, shows that positive emotions are 'resource builders' and they therefore have a long-lasting effect on our personal growth and development. Positive emotion does much more than just feel pleasant – it also has the capacity to broaden and build our psychological and social resources, promote our physical health, connect us to others and build intellectual and psychological reserves. It increases our capacity to be outward looking and pay attention and notice what is happening around us, and increases our working memory, verbal fluency and openness to information.

## The sparkle of good feelings

'Positivity', explains Fredrickson, 'feels good. It's the sparkle of good feelings that awakens your motivation to change' (Fredrickson 2009, p.9). Positivity refers to the whole range of positive emotions to include joy, gratitude, serenity, interest, hope, pride, amusement, awe, inspiration and love. Building a robust Losada ratio (i.e. having more positive thoughts than negative thoughts) and having positive emotions more frequently than negative emotions builds psychological and social capital.

## Effective learners

Thanks to positive psychology and developments in neuroscience the connection between education and happiness is now increasingly recognised to be mutually reinforcing. Robert Emmons (2007), professor at the University of California and one of the world's leading experts on the psychology of gratitude, writes that education helps people to be happy and happy individuals gain more from education. Emmons' work has confirmed what practitioners have always known intuitively – that happy children typically learn and perform better in the classroom than unhappy children. They are more persistent, focused, creative and better able to get along with their peers and staff. Learning associated with positive emotions and well-being is retained whereas learning that is associated with negative emotions – stress, boredom, confusion and low motivation – detract from the learning process.

Neuro-imaging and measurement of brain chemicals now enable us to measure what happens in the brain during the emotional states associated with raised affective filters. Specialised brain scans measure glucose, oxygen use and blood flow in identifiable regions of the brain directly correlated with brain cell (i.e. neural) activity. These show that under stressful emotional conditions sensory input is blocked from entering the brain's prefrontal areas of memory storage so that information is not processed into memory. In other words, when the brain's affective filters are activated by stress, information flow to the prefrontal cortex stops. All input (i.e. the sound of language, the written word) is lost and learning does not take place. There is now a hard science that proves the negative impact on the brain of stress and anxiety and the positive influence of joyful learning on cognition and standardised test success. Effective learning takes place when classroom activities are enjoyable and relevant to pupils' lives, interests and experiences.

As practitioners we therefore need to prevent the negative emotional states that can block learning. Too often in schools an emergency response is activated for non-emergency situations such as being late, misplacing resources or failure to complete a task. Continual release of stress hormones automatically places our body in overdrive resulting in a depleted immune system and a cycle of exacerbated stress. We need to actively promote positive emotional states such as calmness and a sense of well-being that facilitate effective learning.

## Change the subject; think about others not ourselves

When asked what in two words or fewer positive psychology is about Christopher Peterson, one of its founders, replied, 'other people'. Seligman (2011, p.20) writes that 'very little that is positive is solitary...other people are the best antidote to the downs of life and the single most reliable up.' Research by Seligman (2003) has identified that how satisfied you are with your life depends, above all else, on how connected you feel to other people; depth of involvement with family and friends, engagement in satisfying activities and fun leisure activities that take our minds off ourselves are central to achieving happiness. 'Doing' is therefore in Seligman's terms far more productive in terms of flourishing than 'having'. Cool possessions do not bring long-term happiness whereas being connected to others and being engaged in purposeful and meaningful activities does.

Psychologists Ed Diener and Martin Seligman (2002) studied more than two hundred people for months on end, administering tests to determine who was genuinely happy. The happiest people were much more satisfied with their lives for most of the time. They were seldom sad for long when things went wrong, nor were they overwhelmed by euphoria when things went well. Above all, happy people had more friends and spent less time alone. People who say that they have more than five friends are nearly 50 per cent more inclined to feel they are 'very happy' than those who have fewer than five friends. Spending meaningful time with others is vital for our happiness. Friendship, according to the seventeenth century philosopher Francis Bacon, '...redoubleth joys and cutteth grief in half.' 'Without friends no-one would choose to live, though he had all other goods' (Aristotle 350 BC).

## Active constructive responding

Inevitably, then, positive psychologists are concerned with how to turn a good relationship into an excellent one. Shelly Gable, professor at the University of California, and colleagues (Gable *et al.* 2004) have demonstrated that how an individual celebrates with others is more predictive of strong relations than how than how they fight. People we care about often tell us about the good things that happen to them – both the triumphs and the day-to-day joys. How we respond to them can either build the relationship or undermine it. There are four ways of responding, only one of which builds relationships:

1.  *Active and constructive*: genuine response involving eye contact, smiling, touching.
2.  *Passive and constructive*: little or no active emotional expression.
3.  *Active and destructive*: nonverbal displays of negative emotions.
4.  *Passive and destructive*: nonverbal displays of negative emotions, frowning.

Seligman (2011) suggests that once you start consciously enhancing your active and constructive responses, other people will like you better, spend more time with you and share more personal details of their life with you. You, in turn, feel better about yourself and all this further strengthens the critical skill of active constructive responding.

## Flow

According to Martin Seligman (2011) we can also find happiness in life through engagement in meaningful and purposeful pursuits. In Dan Nettle's terms of 'changing the subject' engagement can be achieved through activities which we find compelling. 'Flow' is a term coined by the psychologist Mihaly Csikszentmihalyi (1990) to describe a state of active involvement in a process. During flow, individuals are completely absorbed in what they are doing so that they lose track of time and are completely unself-conscious. The concept of flow features prominently in the positive psychology literature. Athletes often refer to this experience as 'being in the zone'. Tal Ben-Shahar (2007) writes that during flow we are 'performing at our best, we learn, grow, improve and progress towards our future purpose.' Flow is more likely to occur when the challenge of an activity matches our ability. If the activity is too easy it will not engage us sufficiently. If it is too challenging then we are likely to feel overwhelmed and are likely to give up.

The 24 character strengths and six virtues which are presented in Part II of this book are the supports for engagement. We go into flow when our highest strengths are used to meet the challenges that come our way. Using our signature (highest) character strengths leads to increased positive emotion, more meaning and accomplishment and to better relationships.

According to Mihaly Csikszentmihalyi (1990) the world is chaotic. Finding and constructing order and being engaged in a meaningful and purposeful activity is an essential component of flow. Flow activities can enable us to flourish and grow as individuals. Csikszentmihalyi discovered that the more flow individuals experience the more they flourish. This suggests that the key to well-being is about being engaged in the here and now and that happiness is a process rather than an outcome.

In the programme students are introduced to the concept of flow and explore a range of activities from their own experience that generate flow. The importance of finding activities that they can become passionate about is emphasised. Experiencing flow enables individuals to feel more energised and this enthusiasm and energy can carry over into their relationships. Just as apathy pushes people away, being enthusiastic attracts people and can help build friendships. The aim is for students to recognise for themselves that happiness and well-being depend upon the capacity to connect with others and engage in flow experiences.

Engagement is different from positive emotions or happiness because if you ask an individual who is in flow (i.e. fully involved with an absorbing activity) what they are thinking and feeling, they usually say 'nothing' because in flow we merge with the activity and our concentrated attention uses up all our thoughts and feelings. Time flies.

Seligman (2011) writes that there are no shortcuts to flow. Individuals need to use their highest strengths and talents in order to meet the world in flow. Although there are lots of shortcuts to feeling positive emotion, for a while at least – for example, shopping or watching television – there are no shortcuts to flow. Hence the importance of enabling young people to identify their highest or signature strengths and enabling them to use them more often in order to achieve flow.

## Meaningful activity

The quest for engagement and the chase of pleasure are frequently solitary pursuits. Human beings, however, usually want meaning and purpose in their life. This comes from belonging to and serving something that is bigger than ourselves. Positive institutions such as religion, the family and charitable organisations can provide the meaning that we search for in life.

## Signature strengths

Understanding and using our signature (higher) strengths is a key concept in positive psychology and as such underpins all other positive psychology concepts and skills. Our strengths are capacities to think, feel and behave in certain ways. They represent what is best about us. Positive psychologists provide evidence for the fact that strengths can be built and developed and that they underpin good character formation. Using our strengths boosts mood and resilience, increases our well-being and makes us more successful at what we do. Jennifer Fox Eades, programme director for schools and young people at the not-for-profit Centre for Applied Psychology and author of *Celebrating Strengths: Building Strengths-based Schools*, emphasises that 'when we use our strengths we are energised, sparkle and soar. We achieve the highest goals of which we are capable of achieving' (Fox Eades 2008, p.34). The aim of the programme in Part II of this resource aims to enable young people to identify their signature strengths and increase the use of these strengths in their daily lives.

## Building a strengths-based approach

As discussed earlier in this chapter, a great deal of what happens in schools involves focusing on weaknesses: finding out what is wrong and fixing it. The bad news is, however, that when individuals are asked to work more on their weaknesses rather than on their strengths they are likely to lose motivation and become disaffected. Timothy Hodges and Donald Clifton (2004) explain that there may be a better way and that building a strengths-based approach is more productive. The field of neuroscience underpins this finding. Between the ages of three and fifteen, the human brain organises itself by strengthening the synaptic connections that are used most often, while infrequently used connections weaken over time.

Psychologists make a comparison with roads to make this scientific fact more accessible. They suggest that just as roads with the most traffic get widened while the ones that are rarely used fall into disrepair, similarly stronger synapses within the network of connections in the brain continue to strengthen, while weaker connections fade away. After about fifteen years of age, however, an individual's unique network of synaptic connections does not change significantly.

This does not imply, of course, that people cannot change, as individuals can continue to develop a heightened self-awareness, they can stabilise their values and beliefs and they can add knowledge and skills on the way to developing their talents into strengths. However, it seems that the greatest return on an individual's investment into their personal growth comes from focusing on the synaptic connections that are already strong.

Building on this premise, Richard Sternberg (1998) discovered that identifying our strengths and using them in new ways increases our well-being and decreases depressive symptoms. He developed what he calls 'successful intelligence' and suggests that we should spend as little time as possible on our weaknesses and instead focus on developing our strengths.

Ilona Boniwell (2006) writes that strengths are at the core of the positive psychology agenda because they relate to understanding the plus side of the life equation – the presence of psychological health rather than the absence of psychological illness. Psychiatrists and clinical psychologists share a common resource called the DSM (Diagnostic and Statistical Manual; American Psychiatric Association 2000). This reference book contains a classification of mental illness and provides a vocabulary for those working in the field. Symptoms of a variety of mental illnesses – for example, schizophrenia, personality disorder and psychopathic tendencies – are described in detail to allow the professionals to measure what is wrong with a person. Christopher Peterson and Martin Seligman created a corresponding manual of health called the VIA (Values in Action) Classification of Strengths and Virtues. Boniwell (2006) writes that this manual is jokingly referred to as the 'un-DSM' and explains that this classification is based on several assumptions:

- Human strengths are not secondary to weaknesses.
- We can understand human strengths scientifically.
- Human strengths are individual differences between people.

- Human strengths are similar to traits, but can also be influenced by environmental factors.

Strengths such as integrity, fairness and loyalty are the psychological characteristics or moral traits through which we honour and express what we value in life; how we actively integrate who we are with what we value. Strengths are at the very core of the agenda of positive psychology, because they relate to understanding the positive aspects of life – that is, psychological health rather than the absence of psychological illness. Seligman and Peterson standardised the concepts of virtues and strengths. They looked across three thousand years of history, culture, nations and religions and identified the key character strengths from all of them. Faced with hundreds of character strengths they applied several criteria in order to distil the main strengths which they believed to be universal. These criteria include:

- A strength contributes to fulfilment of the good life for a person and others around him or her.

- It is morally valued in its own right, irrespective of whether or not it leads to beneficial outcomes.

- Displaying the strengths does not diminish others, but benefits them, causing admiration rather than jealousy.

- A strength cannot have an opposite that can also be seen as good.

- A strength must show up in a range of a person's behaviours, thoughts, feelings and actions. It should be generalisable across situations and times.

This process resulted in the identification of 24 character strengths that allow us to achieve virtues (which are the core universal characteristics emphasised by both philosophers and religious leaders). These character strengths, organised into six virtues, are listed below (adapted from Peterson and Seligman 2004).

## Values in action character strengths

1. *Wisdom and knowledge*: strengths which are all about learning and using new knowledge:
   - Creativity: thinking of new and interesting ways to do things.
   - Curiosity: taking an interest in what is going on in the world and wanting to find out about new things.
   - Openmindedness: thinking things through carefully before making up your mind, weighing up all the evidence carefully, being able to change your mind when you get new information.
   - Love of learning: learning new skills and information and enjoying finding out more about the things that you already know.
   - Perspective: being wise and looking at the world in a way that makes sense, being able to give others good advice.

2. *Courage*: emotional strengths and being able to overcome difficulties and reach one's goal:

   - Authenticity: speaking the truth, being genuine and true to yourself.

   - Bravery: speaking up for what is right, not running away when things get difficult.

   - Persistence: finishing what you start, keeping going even if things are difficult, enjoying finishing tasks.

   - Zest: approaching life with excitement and energy; not doing things halfway; living life as an adventure; feeling alive and activated.

3. *Humanity*: interpersonal strengths, looking out for and being a being a friend to others:

   - Kindness: helping others and taking care of them.

   - Love: enjoying being close to people.

   - Social intelligence: understanding what makes other people tick, knowing how to fit in and behave in lots of different situations.

4. *Justice*: dealing fairly with people:

   - Fairness: treating all people fairly and giving everybody a fair chance.

   - Leadership: encouraging your team or group to get things done, organising activities and making sure that they happen.

   - Teamwork: working well as a member of a team, being loyal to the group, doing your share.

5. *Temperance*: not overdoing things:

   - Forgiveness: forgiving those who have done wrong, giving people a second chance.

   - Modesty: not 'bigging' yourself up, not seeking the spotlight, not thinking that you are more special than you are.

   - Prudence: making careful choices, not taking big risks, not saying or doing things that you will later regret.

   - Self-regulation: controlling your behaviour, not being too emotional, not eating too much.

6. *Transcendence*: strengths that make connections to the universe and provide meaning in life:

   - Appreciation of beauty and excellence: noticing and appreciating beauty and things done well – that is, skills and talents.

   - Gratitude: being aware of and thankful for the good things that happen to you; taking time to say thank you.

   - Hope: expecting the best in the future and working towards it, believing that a good future is something that can be built.

— Humour: liking to laugh and play; bringing smiles to other people, sharing a joke and a laugh.

— Religiousness: having beliefs about the meaning of the universe and about life that shape one's behaviour and provide comfort.

To find your character strengths, log onto www.authentichappiness.com, VIA (values in action) signature strengths questionnaire.

Note that not all positive psychologists working with strengths are doing so from a 'values' perspective. The Clifton Strengths Finder, for example, consists of a longer list that is more focused on business skills.

At the Centre for Applied Positive Psychology website (www.cappeu.com) you can take a comprehensive test for a small fee. This assessment tool allows you to identify many top strengths, as well as highlighting the strengths you don't use enough and those that you could pay more attention to.

Playing to one's strengths is recognised as being the best way to handle challenging situations, and by applying one's strengths creatively we can increase our happiness resilience and thus a sense of well-being. Research by Clifton and Anderson (2002) suggests that knowing and following one's strengths:

- encourages insight and perspective in one's life

- generates optimism

- provides a sense of direction

- helps to develop confidence

- generates a sense of vitality

- brings a sense of fulfilment

- helps achieve one's goals.

According to Martin Seligman you are using a character strength when:

- what you are doing feels authentic and gives you a sense of your real self

- you feel excited

- there is and has been a rapid learning curve involved

- it offers new ways to use existing skills

- you long to be/do this

- there is an inevitability about doing this and you feel unable to stop yourself from doing it

- you feel invigorated rather than depleted doing it

- you find yourself engaging in activities and projects that require you to be this way

- you feel joy and enthusiasm.

(Seligman 2003, p.160)

When we are behaving in a way that meets the criteria above, Seligman believes we are using our 'signature character strengths'. A strength is defined in two ways: firstly as a trait (i.e. an underlying psychological characteristic) and secondly as something valued in its own right, desired as a quality for nothing but itself.

Seligman goes as far as to suggest that we can only flourish when we are using our signature character strengths. At such times we are more likely to be engaged in what we are doing and therefore feel energised and enjoy what we are doing. A strengths approach runs against the received wisdom that we should not talk about our strengths for fear of appearing to be boastful and instead we should concentrate on addressing our shortcomings. Peterson and Seligman (2004) argue fiercely against this position on two counts. First, they challenge the view that everybody can learn to be competent in almost anything. Second, they challenge the view that the greatest potential for growth is an individual's areas of greatest weakness.

Using our strengths is crucial to our well-being because they enable us to be motivated and achieve our goals. Often we love a context because we have the opportunity to engage in and use our strengths in support of what we value. A study by positive psychologist Alex Linley and colleagues (Linley *et al.* 2010) confirms that people who use their strengths are more likely to achieve their goals as well as feel more fulfilled and happy with those goals. This resource is designed to provide practitioners with practical ideas for increasing and developing young people's awareness of their individual strengths and enable them to experience the power and the joy of using them. As Jenny Fox Eades (2008, p.10) writes, 'you get more of what you focus on, so focus on your strengths!'

## The development of signature strengths

In his book *Authentic Happiness* (2003) Martin Seligman describes how the development of strengths in young children is like the development of language. Most newborns have the capacity for every human language and the attentive listener will hear the basic sounds of each language in the baby's earliest babbling. However, what Seligman calls 'babbling drift' sets in. The infant's babbling 'drifts' more and more towards the language spoken by the people in the environment; thus by the end of the first year of life, the baby's vocalisations resemble the sounds of the 'mother-tongue-to-be'. Seligman suggests that similarly healthy newborns also have the capacity for each of the 24 strengths; however, 'strengthening drift' sets in over the first six years of life. As young children find the niches that bring praise, love and attention, they sculpt their strengths accordingly. Their chisels are the 'interplay of talents, interests and strengths' and as a child discovers what works and what does not work he will 'carve in great detail the face of several strengths and at the same time he will chip others out, discarding the excess granite on the art-room floor' (p.245).

## Building signature strengths

Seligman's (2003) advice for building strengths in children and young people is twofold and is equally applicable to home and school. First, it is important to reward all displays of any of the character strengths. Eventually you will discover the young person drifting in the direction of a few of them. These are what Seligman terms the 'seed crystals' of the individual's signature strengths. Second, Seligman emphasises the importance of creating opportunities for the young person to display these developing strengths throughout the daily routine. When they are displayed, it is important to acknowledge them with a name.

The work of Peterson and Seligman (2004) emphasises that strengths can be built and developed and that they underpin good character formation. We love to use our strengths and the process of identifying and using them boosts mood and resilience, increases our flourishing or well-being and enables us to be more successful at what we do. Using our character strengths is how we express what we value and need emotionally in our life, and using them in new ways can have a lasting effect on increasing our happiness and reducing symptoms of depression. Strengths are the psychological characteristics through which we honour and express what we value in life, and how we actively integrate who we are with what we value.

## Strengths and talents

Although strengths and talents are both key topics in positive psychology and have many similarities in common, there are also a number of important differences. First, strengths are moral traits whereas talents are 'non-moral'. Second, although both strengths and talents can be built on in a significant way, character strengths are far more 'buildable' than talents and with practice, persistence, good teaching and dedication they can take root and flourish.

When it comes to talent, you can improve on your ability to, for example, sing in tune, but the level of improvement may not be significant when compared with one's baseline abilities. Martin Seligman (2003, p.134) clarifies this essential difference between strengths and talents when he writes:

> ...true, you can improve your time in the hundred-metre dash by raising your rump higher in the starting position, you can wear makeup that makes you look prettier or you can listen to a great deal of classical music and learn to guess the pitch correctly more often. I believe that these are only small improvements, though, and about augmenting a talent that already exists. There is a ceiling therefore on how much of a talent you can acquire and what you acquire is a mere 'simulacrum' or resemblance of the talent rather than the real thing. This, however, is not true of strengths; when you acquire a strength you have the real thing.

Talents, unlike strengths, are largely innate. Of course they involve some choices, but the choices are in the context of choosing whether to use and develop the talent rather than about possessing that talent in the beginning. Talents are abilities that are brought to the surface when we begin to use them when pursuing various activities. Hence the importance of encouraging young children to engage in a variety of experiences so that they have opportunities to discover their talents. For example, some very young children naturally have good hand-eye coordination which make them very good at being able to do things such as hit a ball. This talent can be enhanced to the point of exceptional ability. Malcolm Gladwell (2009) suggests, however, that this requires ten thousand hours of practice before the age of 18 years.

Strengths, on the other hand, are personality traits that can be acquired through active intentions such as practising, reading about them or learning from others. Just because we were not born with certain personality traits doesn't mean we can't develop them. For example it is possible to train oneself to be diligent, patient, kind. Strengths can be acquired by almost any individual as long as there is time, effort and commitment.

Strengths are therefore usually far more voluntary; there are many choices when it comes to strengths. You can decide whether you want to have a particular strength, whether you want to use it and develop a strength even further, whether to keep building it and to some extent whether to acquire it in the beginning, Also strengths cannot be squandered.

## 'Strengthspotting'

This significant finding is the foundation stone that underpins the programme which is described in this book. Chris Peterson, a leading researcher in character strengths in youth, claims that being able to name what one does well is intriguing and even empowering (Peterson 2006). By learning about their strengths and ways to use and build upon them students can be encouraged to acknowledge, own and use the strengths and therefore create for themselves the opportunity to flourish. 'Strengthspotting' is a term coined by positive psychologist Alex Linley (2008). Linley suggests that only 30 per cent of us have a meaningful understanding of what our strengths are and he suggests that we ought to spend more time identifying them in order to flourish.

Building up a young person's personal resources is a vital part of building resilience. A well-resourced individual has more to call on to help them when the going gets tough. Psychologist Michael Ungar (2006) explains that the factors that contribute to an individual's resilience combine exponentially; that is, they don't just build one on top of the other. The more there are, the greater the effect. Having one characteristic that bolsters resilience is good. Two is even better but the real difference comes when we start having three. Three resources are experienced as if we have four. If we have four characteristics or resources that make us resilient, it is the equivalent of having eight good things to say about ourselves.

## Golden seeds

It is vital that we are open to the talents and strengths that our students possess or wish to develop. In his book *Average to A+*, Alex Linley writes about the responsibility practitioners have to identify what he calls young people's 'golden seeds'. This means noticing, commenting on and commending strengths in young people. As Handy describes it:

> A golden seed…refers to the way someone can often in our formative years, notice an aptitude or talent and pick it out, comment on it, often just in a chance remark. We tuck away this expression of confidence in us and when the time comes, we dig up this seed, water it and prove it true. Often the most memorable thing a teacher can do is give us our golden seed. (Handy, cited in Linley 2008, p.245)

## Leaden seeds

The opposite of the 'golden seed' is the 'leaden seed', the unnecessarily negative and critical remarks which can lead us to believe that we cannot do something. This sort of belief can be extremely damaging and debilitating.

Thanks to positive psychology there is now a body of knowledge verified by science that can inform us how to live a fulfilling life. It emphasises the value of relationships, meaning and engagement and plays down the importance of consumerism. Happiness or flourishing in western societies has been found to be only weakly affected by demographic characteristics such as wealth and material possessions. Research by Martin Seligman (2003) has identified that depth of involvement with family and friends, engagement in satisfying activities and being able to use our signature strengths are central to achieving happiness. Well-being is important not just because it feels good but because it creates better commerce with the world. Happy people are healthier, harder working and more involved with family, friends and the community. There is increasing evidence that happiness is a powerful preventative and remedial 'medicine' as well as something that enables us to flourish.

## Positive psychology: key concepts and skills

Here we present a number of the key strategies from positive psychology to support facilitators with the process of delivering the programme. They include:

- mindfulness
- appreciative enquiry
- three good things exercise
- active gratitude
- acts of random kindness.

These activities have been selected on the basis that they form the building blocks of a 'strengths' approach and can be easily incorporated in to the programme thus enhancing the facilitator's repertoire of strengths-based interventions.

### *Mindfulness*

Mindfulness is a key strategy from positive psychology and it is one that practitioners can usefully employ regularly as a 'ritual' at the beginning of each day or lesson as a way of alleviating anxiety, establishing calm and thereby getting each session off to a positive start. Mindfulness is about being calm, not thinking about the past or worrying about the future but being available to attend to the here and now. It has shown to have benefits for health and happiness and improve mood. Since positive emotion and a calm inner state help us to learn more effectively it is an important life skill that students can use in other situations if they wish.

Psychologists have demonstrated that when our slow, deep outgoing breath is longer than our slow, incoming breath, our nervous system is stimulated bringing about a sense of relaxation. Neurobiologists offer a straightforward explanation to the value of mindfulness based on the rest principle. It suggests that actively used neurological connections will become stronger if they are allowed to rest briefly. Mindfulness involves intentional resting and thereby triggers a follow-up quickening or deepening of certain neurological processes. Immediate changes include a feeling of relaxation, a heightened self-awareness and feelings of calm. Changes that endure over time include improved concentration, empathy and perceptual acuity, lowered levels of stress and anxiety and more effective performance in a broad range of domains from sports and academic tests and creativity.

Attention is the name that psychologists give to our capacity to focus on a particular line of thought or task. It is like a spotlight in the head that can be focused at will on a thought or task activity. Practitioners know that a student's ability to direct and maintain attention on a task has a direct effect on successful learning. Mindfulness is therefore a key strategy to use throughout the programme as it has the proven capacity to nourish the quality of one's attention.

It is important to introduce students to mindfulness as part of the well-being programme to promote calming practices in the classroom that will improve attention and mood and assist learning.

## PRACTICAL TECHNIQUES FOR DEVELOPING MINDFULNESS

### Mind in a jar

This exercise, devised by MacLean (2004), is useful to use with students who are new to mindfulness and have difficulty paying attention as the process involves movement that has the capacity to hold one's attention. It involves filling a glass jar with water and noticing how the jar of clear water is like one's mind during a quiet moment.

The next step is to take a small handful of sand or soil and place it in the jar and suggest to the students that each one of the tiny grains of either soil or sand represents a thought; exciting thoughts, happy thoughts, angry thoughts. Put a lid on the jar and shake it up, so that everything swirls around faster and faster. The swirling contents of the jar represent one's mind in a hurry.

Now let everything calm down by letting the jar sit still on the table. This is one's mind during the process of mindfulness. Watch the thoughts settle down to the bottom, leaving the water – that is, one's mind – light and clear again. Now it is possible to think clearly and pay attention.

### Mantras

Using a mantra to achieve calmness involves choosing a word and repeating it in one's mind, slowly and thoughtfully. Notice when one's mind wanders and bring it quietly back to the word. It will be helpful in terms of encouraging students to become familiar with the 24 signature strengths that form the backbone of this programme to use the strength that is being introduced or alternatively ask individual students to use one of their signature strengths as a mantra.

## Appreciative enquiry

Appreciative enquiry is one of the key concepts of positive psychology. This is an innovative and simple approach to change and a process that encapsulates many of the core values of positive psychology. It was originally developed by Cooperrider (2001). It can be summed up by the phrase, 'What Works Well'. Its acronym WWW makes the term highly memorable.

Appreciative enquiry builds on what is termed the 'neuroplasticity' of the brain – its ability to grow and develop right into old age. Neuroscientists have discovered that positive thoughts create deeper, stronger channels that consequently enable future positive thoughts to come more easily. The same, however, is true for negative thoughts so that the more negative thoughts an individual has the easier it is to think negatively in the future.

The process of appreciative enquiry involves first focusing on what works or has worked well in situations, for example in relationships, organisations and communities, rather than what hasn't worked. The process therefore starts with discovering what it was that created success, capability or effectiveness in specific situations. Second, it involves asking why it worked. Tal Ben-Shahar (2007, p.139) suggests that, '…by inquiring into positive past experiences we can learn from them and then apply our learning to present and future situations.'

The process of appreciative enquiry is based on principles of equality as everyone involved is asked to express their thoughts, and its goal is to create organisations that are in full voice. It involves the art and practice of asking questions that focus on strengthening positive potential.

Appreciative enquiry is a useful strategy for facilitators to employ when delivering the programme. Martin Seligman (2011) believes that being in touch with what we do well underpins our readiness to change. Criticism, on the other hand, too frequently makes individuals feel helpless and dig in our heels so that we don't change. We do change, however, when we explore what is best about ourselves and when we see specific ways to use our strengths.

## Three good things exercise

This exercise, sometimes called 'the happiness journal' (MacConville 2009), involves students recording three good things that have happened to them in the course of the day or week, depending how often they do the activity. The three good things can be small in importance ('I had my favourite chocolate pudding for lunch today') or more significant ('My dad came home from work early today to spend time with me'). Next to each 'good thing' students are asked to write out the answer to one of the following questions:

- Why did this good thing happen?
- What does this mean to you?
- How can you have more of this good thing in the future?

The challenge of this apparently simple exercise is to be able to focus specifically on things and events that we have enjoyed in the here and now. Essentially this exercise works by re-educating our attention to look for what is good in life.

## Active gratitude

Martin Seligman (2011) has suggested that doing the three good things exercise regularly can make you measurably happier. It seems that the act of counting your blessings somehow makes them appear to multiply. Emmons (2007) in his book aptly entitled *Thanks* suggests that it is helpful to think of gratitude first as the acknowledgement of goodness in one's life, and second, recognising that the sources of this goodness lie at least partially outside the self. It involves a focus on the present moment and focusing on the things that an individual has rather than things they do not have.

Essentially this exercise works by re-educating attention to look for what is good in life. A habit grows from repeated action, creating neural networks in our brains that can direct our attention without conscious thought. This activity works by encouraging individuals to notice and be aware of the 'good things' in their lives and to focus regularly on happy moments. A 'good thing' might be as small as appreciating a delicious piece of chocolate. Emmons suggests that individuals who practise active gratitude are happier, more energetic and experience more frequent, positive emotions. This is because they learn to notice the positive things that happen to them every day and thus make the connection that it is the small, seemingly insignificant moments in their lives that make the big picture of their lives work. By learning to notice and enjoy the sources of happiness here and now students learn that they can create a life with even more capacity to enjoy tomorrow. Also, the more an individual is inclined towards active gratitude the less likely that individual is to be depressed, anxious, lonely or envious.

## Random acts of kindness

We can enhance our positive emotion and well-being by increasing our kindness. Random acts of kindness involve finding one completely, unexpected thing to do and just doing it. This is because acts of kindness employ our strengths. Sonja Lyubomirsky, professor in psychology at the University of California, suggests that being kind is about investing in social connections and being kind and generous leads us to perceive others more positively and more charitably. In Dan Nettle's (2005) terms it shifts the focus from ourselves to others, which is a key activity for building happiness. When we commit acts of kindness we begin to view ourselves as a selfless and compassionate person. This new identity can promote a sense of confidence, optimism about our ability to help and our usefulness. It also highlights our own abilities, resources and expertise and brings a feeling of enhanced control into our lives. Acts of kindness can also promote a sense of meaningfulness and value in one's life because they inspire greater liking by others as well as appreciation and gratitude.

We learn to be kind by being kind. Random acts of kindness are behaviours that benefit others or make others happy, usually at some cost to ourselves, and are unexpected. Random acts of kindness are not about duty or obligation and can be small and brief (e.g. giving a stranger who is short of change coins in the supermarket, letting a person who is obviously under time pressure go in front of you in the canteen).

Sonja Lyubomirsky (2007) provides some advice on how to ensure this strategy is successful:

1. Timing is everything. Doing random acts of kindness over and above what we are used to doing will give us a boost in well-being. If we do them too infrequently we will not feel any benefit; if we do them too often it is likely that we will end up feeling overburdened.

2. Vary what you do. If you repeat the same thing it will become a habit and will no longer bring the same level of positive emotion. This is not to say stop doing what you have been doing, but add new acts of kindness to your repertoire and increase effort and creativity.

3. On a weekly basis, do more of what does not come naturally. Sonja Lyubomirsky suggests this might, for example, involve being courteous to 'cold callers'.

4. Work to increase compassion – one's willingness and ability to empathise. Put yourself in another's shoes and listen carefully to their point of view.

5. On a weekly basis do a kind deed about which you tell no one and don't expect anything in return. This, suggests Sonja Lyubomirsky, will deepen your sense of value, meaning and self-worth.

Acts of kindness have positive social consequences because they create a ripple effect. The recipient may be cheered, surprised or comforted and your random act of kindness may motivate that person to return the favour to other individuals who in turn may be kind the next day. Also, witnessing or even hearing about a kindness leads people to increase their motivation to be kind to others themselves.

# POWERPOINT PRESENTATION

This section contains notes to support the facilitator in delivering a PowerPoint presentation of 20 slides. The purpose of the presentation is to introduce staff to the main principles of positive psychology and to provide practitioners with a guide to delivering the programme.

The PowerPoint slides are available at:
www.jkp.com/catalogue/book/9781849052610/resources

In preparation for the session participants should take 20 minutes to find their VIA (Values in Action) character strengths at www.authentichappiness.com, VIA signature strengths questionnaire.

## SLIDE 1

### Building Happiness, Resilience and Motivation in Adolescents

## Facilitator's notes

The aim of this presentation is twofold. First, it will introduce staff to the main principles of positive psychology and introduce a 'strengths approach' to building young people's well-being and achievement. Second, it will provide practitioners with a guide to delivering the programme.

### SLIDE 2

**What is Positive Psychology?**

Positive psychology is an umbrella term for the study of positive emotions and positive character traits. It is concerned with what makes people flourish, that is, become happier, more connected to others and engaged in purposeful, meaningful activity.

It was launched as a new discipline in 1998 by Martin Seligman, the then president of the American Psychological Association.

Research findings from positive psychology are not meant to replace traditional psychology and what is known about human suffering, weakness and disorder. The aim is to have a complete and balanced understanding of the human experience.

## Facilitator's notes

The main thrust of positive psychology is to redress the traditional focus of psychology that concentrates on human weakness, suffering and disorder. It therefore examines 'what works well' rather than 'what doesn't work' or is 'broken'.

Positive psychology is not a specialist discipline within psychology. It is an approach to how psychology is practised. Any psychologist is practising as a positive psychologist if that practitioner is using a 'strengths' approach and focusing on 'what works well'.

Research within this field has grown considerably over the past decade and there is now considerable data verifying the substantial control that individuals have over their happiness and well-being. Perhaps the most recognised aspect of positive psychology is the new science of happiness.

## Activity

Provide an opportunity for participants to ask questions and/or seek clarification on positive psychology.

### SLIDE 3

**Building a 'Strengths Approach'**

A strengths approach focusing on 'what works well' and individual strengths and talents works at three levels:

1.  the individual level, whether that is the individual staff member or student

2.  the classroom or class group level

3.  the whole school level.

Ideally all three levels will work together; however, small changes at the individual level can have a positive effect – small differences can make a big difference.

## Facilitator's notes

A strengths approach is one where the focus is primarily on strengths not weaknesses, and where both staff and students aim not to be 'OK' but to excel. An important component of enabling individuals to flourish is through enabling them to identify their character strengths and strengthen them by using them in new ways.

Filling our physical environment with positive words and images, putting effort into creating a peaceful, attractive environment and using the language of strengths in our day-to-day contacts will help to ensure that relationships within the school are positive and affirming.

## Activity

Ask participants to discuss in pairs what the term 'strengths approach' means to them in the context of their work and to explore the ways in which they can build this approach into their day-to-day work.

Ask for feedback.

### SLIDE 4

**'Subjective Well-being' is the Scientific Term for Happiness**

Well-being has five measurable elements (PERMA) (Seligman 2011):

1. positive emotion, of which happiness and life satisfaction are aspects
2. engagement
3. relationships
4. meaning
5. achievement.

## Facilitator's notes

The terms well-being, happiness and flourishing are for the purposes of this resource interchangeable. However, in the positive psychology literature there are some recognised differences in their meanings. Seligman has recently announced that his thinking has moved on and he now 'detests the word *happiness*, which is so overused that it has become almost meaningless.' He suggests that it is an unworkable term for science, or for any practical goal such as education or changing your personal life, because the modern ear immediately hears 'happy' to mean good mood, good cheer and smiling. Seligman now considers that the main topic of positive psychology is well-being not happiness. Happiness is now considered to be only part of well-being. The gold standard for measuring well-being is flourishing.

## Activity

Provide an opportunity for participants to ask questions and/or seek clarification on the terms 'happiness' and 'well-being'.

---

### SLIDE 5

**What is Flourishing?**

To flourish an individual needs the three core features of well-being (Felicia Huppert and Timothy So, quoted in Seligman 2011):

1.  positive emotion (or happiness)
2.  engagement and interest
3.  meaning and purpose

and three of the six additional features:

1.  self-esteem
2.  optimism
3.  resilience
4.  vitality
5.  self-determination
6.  positive relationships.

---

## Facilitator's notes

Based on Seligman's recent rethink of positive psychology:

*   well-being has taken centre stage
*   happiness is now only part of the bigger picture of well-being
*   flourishing is the outcome of well-being.

There are of course those who would disagree with Seligman's rethink of the term 'happiness'. Aristotle rejected the idea that happiness is only about pleasure and argued that the aim of life should be 'eudemonia'– that is, meaningful. For the purposes of the programme, therefore, the three key terms well-being, happiness and flourishing are interchangeable with the understanding that it is quality of our inner life rather than materialism that constitutes happiness.

## Activity

Provide an opportunity for participants to ask questions/seek clarification on the terms:

*   well-being
*   happiness
*   flourishing.

Ask participants to choose a young person they work with and think about which of the features of 'flourishing' this young person demonstrates.

Take feedback.

---

## SLIDE 6

### What You Can Do to Get Well-being

The task of positive psychology is to *describe* not *prescribe* what people can do to get well-being. The findings can be neatly summarised (adapted from Nettle 2005) as:

- Increasing positive emotions.
- Reducing the impact of negative emotions.
- Changing the subject: thinking about others rather than ourselves and engaging in purposeful activity.
- Finding meaning in one's life.

---

## Facilitator's notes

Positive psychologists have shown that we can make ourselves happier by:

- focusing on positive thoughts
- consciously reducing negative thoughts
- increasing our connection to other people
- involving ourselves in enjoyable and purposeful activities
- serving a goal which is bigger than ourselves – for example, family or religion.

This list sums up many of the key concepts in positive psychology. Each of the six items on this list is an important component of happiness or flourishing and is verified by a huge body of research.

Thanks to positive psychologists there is now a body of knowledge that can inform us how to live a fulfilling life. In contrast to the widespread view that it is money and possessions that make us happy this data emphasises the value of relationships, meaning and engagement. Clearly a certain amount of money is necessary to provide security and protect us from poverty and lack of medical care; however, if an individual has enough cash to live on, the chances that merely having more money will make an individual happier are close to zero.

## Activity

Ask participants to consider the implications of these findings for their work.

Take feedback.

## SLIDE 7

### Increase Positive Emotions

The 'Broaden-and-Build' theory of positive emotions developed by Barbara Fredrickson (2009) shows that positive emotions are 'resource builders' and have a long-lasting effect on our personal growth and development. Positive emotions have the capacity to broaden and build our psychological and social resources, promote our physical health, connect us to others and build our intellectual and psychological reserves. They increase our capacity to be outward looking and pay attention and notice what is happening around us, and increase our working memory, verbal fluency and openness to information.

## Facilitator's notes

Barbara Fredrickson's 'Broaden-and-Build' theory of positive emotions explains the contributions of positive emotion to human well-being and flourishing. Whereas negative emotions such as fear and anger lead to narrow responses based on avoiding threat, positive emotions 'broaden and build' or increase our intellectual processes. Individuals in a positive mood:

- have a broader focus of attention
- generate more ideas
- are more resilient in stressful situations
- are more generous and tolerant.

## Activity

As practitioners we know intuitively that happy students enjoy learning and are generally more successful in school than their less contented peers. Ask participants to discuss as a group what they can do to 'broaden and build' positive emotions in the students they work with.

Take feedback and note down suggestions.

## SLIDE 8

### The Sparkle of Good Feelings

'Positivity' triggers the sparkle of good feelings that awakens an individual's inspiration and motivation to change.

Positivity refers to the whole range of positive emotions to include joy, gratitude, serenity, interest, hope, pride, amusement, awe, inspiration and love.

Building a robust Losada ratio (i.e. having more positive thoughts than negative thoughts) and having positive emotions more frequently than negative emotions builds psychological and social capital.

## Facilitator's notes

'Positivity' increases our confidence and leads us to have an increased repertoire of behaviours:

- joy leads to play
- pride leads us to dream big
- interest leads us to explore
- gratitude leads us to creative giving.

## Activity

Ask participants to discuss with their neighbour and agree on and add three further examples of positive emotions and the behaviours that they lead to. Ask participants to base their discussion on personal experience:

1. …………….. leads to ……………..
2. …………….. leads to ……………..
3. …………….. leads to ……………..

Ask for feedback and note down responses.

---

### SLIDE 9

**Flow**

According to Seligman, 'engagement' is an essential component of well-being. Engagement is achieved through flow.

Flow is a term coined by the Russian psychologist Mihaly Csikzentmihalyi (pronounced 'cheeks sent me high') that refers to a state of optimal experience and involvement in an activity during which we are performing at our best.

Flow is:

- being at one with 'the music', that is, an activity that has clear goals
- time stopping
- the loss of self-consciousness during an absorbing activity
- intrinsically rewarding and motivating.

---

## Facilitator's notes

Flow is a central concept in positive psychology. It is about engagement in absorbing and purposeful activities that make us forget time. Flow is different from pleasure – simply doing things that are enjoyable like watching television or shopping – because flow activities are demanding and take up all our attention and concentration. If you ask an individual who is in flow, that is, fully involved with an absorbing activity, what they are thinking and feeling they usually say 'nothing' because in flow we merge with the activity and our concentrated attention uses up all our thoughts and feelings. Time flies.

According to the Russian psychologist Mihaly Csikszentmihalyi, who identified the term, the world is chaotic. Finding and constructing order and being engaged in a meaningful and purposeful activity is an essential component of flow. Flow activities can enable us to flourish.

Individuals need to use their highest character strengths and talents in order to achieve flow. Although there are lots of easy ways of making ourselves feel happy, for example shopping or watching television, there are no shortcuts to flow. Hence the importance of enabling young people to identify their highest or signature strengths and talents and enabling them to use them more often in order to achieve flow.

## Activity

Provide an opportunity for participants to ask questions and/or seek clarification on flow. Ask participants to share their experiences of flow and take feedback on examples of the activities which enable them to achieve flow.

### SLIDE 10

**The Eight Ingredients of Flow**

Mihaly Csikszentmihalyi suggests that flow has the following eight ingredients (adapted from Craig 2007):

1. We are involved in tasks that we have a good chance of completing.
2. We are able to fully concentrate on the activity.
3. The task has clear goals.
4. The task provides immediate feedback on how well we are doing.
5. Our involvement in the task is 'deep but effortless' and this involvement takes away the worries and frustration of everyday life.
6. We have a sense of exercising a sense of control over our actions.
7. 'Concerns for the self disappear' but our 'sense of self emerges stronger after the flow experience is over'.
8. We lose our usual sense of time.

## Facilitator's notes

Flow is an important concept for students to appreciate because the engagement and concentration which are critical elements of flow are the essential triggers for motivation. There are no shortcuts to flow; being in flow depends upon students using their character strengths and talents. If students do not experience flow they are at risk of becoming disaffected. On the other hand there are effortless shortcuts to experiencing positive emotion, that is, pleasure, through shopping, watching TV or taking drugs for example. However, the pleasure that accompanies these pleasures is extremely short-lived. This is because of a process that positive psychologists call 'adaptation' – we get used to the good and the bad things that happen to us. This finding underpins the importance of enabling students to discover their strengths and talents and thus experience flow. Pleasure does not lead to motivation and well-being, flow does.

## Activity

Ask participants to explore how flow can be encouraged in the classroom.
Ask for feedback.

---

### SLIDE 11

**Signature Strengths**

Peterson and Seligman (2004) identified 24 signature (higher) strengths. These are organised into the six virtues which are universal characteristics that are emphasised by philosophers and religious leaders:

1. Wisdom and knowledge
2. Courage
3. Love and humanity
4. Justice
5. Temperance
6. Transcendence.

---

## Facilitator's notes

Traditional psychology revolved around the DSM (Diagnostic and Statistical Manual; American Psychiatric Association 2000), a manual which contains detailed descriptions of *everything* that can go wrong with the human brain and personality. Positive psychology's answer to the DSM is the VIA (Values in Action) Classification of Strengths. It emerged from extensive research by Martin Seligman and Chris Peterson, on what character strengths and virtues consistently emerge from historical and international surveys about what people have always valued about one another.

This work lists universal 'character strengths and virtues' with focus on what is right about people and, most importantly, the strengths of character that make the good life possible. Character strengths are how we express what we value and need emotionally in our lives.

## Activity

Ask participants to read the handout 'Virtues and Character Strengths', and consider how this list relates to:

- building positive relationships with others
- engaging in purposeful activity
- finding meaning in our lives.

Ask for feedback.

## Handout for Slide 11: Virtues and Character Strengths

| | | | |
|---|---|---|---|
| 1. | **Wisdom and knowledge**<br>Curiosity/interest<br>Love of learning<br>Originality/ingenuity/creativity<br>Perspective | 4. | **Justice**<br>Citizenship/duty/loyalty/teamwork<br>Equality/fairness<br>Leadership |
| 2. | **Courage**<br>Valour<br>Industry/perseverance<br>Integrity/honesty<br>Zest/enthusiasm | 5. | **Temperance**<br>Forgiveness/mercy<br>Modesty/humility<br>Self-control/self-regulation<br>Prudence/caution |
| 3. | **Love and humanity**<br>Intimacy<br>Kindness/generosity/nurturance<br>Social intelligence | 6. | **Transcendence**<br>Appreciation of beauty/awe<br>Gratitude<br>Hope/optimism<br>Humour/playfulness<br>Religiousness/sense of purpose |

### SLIDE 12

**Character Strengths and Flow**

When our signature strengths are used to meet the challenge involved in flow activities we feel energised, creative and capable.

The more we can identify and build our character strengths and recognise how we are using them the happier, more energised and effective we will feel.

Being able to put a name to what we do well is intriguing and empowering.

## Facilitator's notes

Character strengths are very 'buildable'.

Recognising and building our strengths is a joyful process that is about self-discovery, creativity and ownership.

## Activity

Ask participants to think about their signature strengths and consider how they are able to use these strengths in their work.

Ask participants to think about how they feel when they are using their strengths.

Ask for feedback, emphasising again that when we use our strengths we feel positive and capable.

### SLIDE 13

**Identify Your Signature Strengths**

Characteristics of signature strengths (adapted from Boniwell 2006):

- They represent the real you.
- They bring a feeling of excitement when they are used.
- A person excels in their signature strengths quickly.
- A person longs to put them into action.
- A person feels energised and intrinsically motivated when using them.
- They can be applied to learning, work, relationships and play.

## Facilitator's notes

When we are using our strengths we are much more likely to be engaged in what we are doing. When we are engaged we are energised and enjoy what we are doing. Using our strengths is therefore an excellent way of becoming motivated, resilient and achieving our goals. This finding from positive psychologists underpins the importance of enabling students to recognise their strengths and talents.

## Activity

Ask participants to think about one of the students they work with and discuss with a partner how the student's strengths and talents show up in their life.

Ask for feedback.

---

**SLIDE 14**

### Why Engaging With Our Strengths and Talents is Important

- Rise in mental health problems.
- The impact of advertising on students' perceptions of themselves and their expectations.
- The growing fear in society as a result of the rise of the threat of terrorism, the recession and increase in unemployment, increase in crime levels and rioting.
- Family/community breakdown, increase of divorce, social isolation.
- Increased expectations and pressures on young people.

---

## Facilitator's notes

The demands of growing up in today's society mean that all young people need to deal with life's challenges and difficulties. Stress and adversity have become an inevitable part of life for us all.

## Activity

Ask participants to consider how engaging with our strengths and talents can enable us to cope with life's challenges and inevitable difficulties.

Ask for feedback.

---

**SLIDE 15**

### Character Strengths and Talents

According to positive psychologists, strengths and talents are both essential for human flourishing. There are, however, important differences between them:

- Strengths are moral traits, talents are non-moral.
- Talents are largely innate, character strengths are more 'voluntary' — we can choose to develop them.
- Strengths cannot be squandered; however, we can choose not to use a talent.

Character strengths are more 'buildable' than talents: with practice, persistence, good teaching and dedication they can take root and flourish. Strengths can be acquired by almost any individual as long as there is time, effort and commitment.

---

## Facilitator's notes

Although character strengths and talents are both essential for human flourishing there are important differences between them.

The programme in this resource builds on the premise that character strengths are 'buildable' and with practice, persistence, good teaching and dedication they can take root and flourish.

This is an optimistic message of hope for practitioners because enabling young people to get in touch with their strengths enables them to become motivated, resilient and achieve their goals.

## Activity

Ask participants to consider the implications for their work of the fact that character strengths are 'buildable'.

### SLIDE 16

**Knowing and Following One's Character Strengths**

Knowing and following one's character strengths (adapted from Clifton and Anderson 2002):

- encourages insight and perspective in one's life
- generates optimism
- provides a sense of direction
- helps to develop optimism
- generates a sense of vitality
- brings a sense of fulfilment
- helps achieve one's goals.

## Facilitator's notes

A 'strengths' approach runs against the received wisdom that we should not talk about our strengths, for fear of being boastful and we should focus on our shortcomings.

## Activity

Ask participants to discuss the implications of working with students' strengths instead of focusing on their weaknesses for their work

### SLIDE 17

**Building Happiness, Resilience and Motivation in Adolescents**

The aim of the programme is to introduce students to the concept of character strengths, enable them to identify their signature (higher) strengths and develop new ways of using them.

The programme is presented in six sections; each section represents one of the six virtues. The virtues are made up of 24 character strengths. There is a chapter or session for each character strength.

## Facilitator's notes

The sessions can be delivered flexibly according to the needs of the students. They can be delivered as whole class sessions, to small groups or to individual students. The sessions should be interactive with an emphasis on discussion, group and partner work.

The sessions can also be delivered to individuals as part of a mentoring, coaching or counselling session.

Each chapter contains a range of activities to ensure student interest and engagement.

## Activity

Provide each participant with a sample session from the programme and allow up to ten minutes for participants to read the session notes.

Provide opportunity for participants to ask questions and seek clarification on the content and structure of the session.

### SLIDE 18

**Delivering the Programme**

The programme relates directly to the students' experiences. It is about enabling young people to experience their character strengths in practice.

The guiding principle should be that the students should be enabled to (adapted from Morris 2009):

1. recognise their character in action
2. reflect on their usefulness for their lives
3. discover new ways of using their signature (higher) strengths.

## Facilitator's notes

Teaching the programme is in many ways like the teaching of other subjects, but with one important difference. The subject is directly about the students themselves rather than being about ideas that are 'academic' which then have to be translated back into something relevant to their lives. The aim of the programme is to enable students to experience something that can then be put into practice in their own lives.

## Activity

Provide an opportunity for participants to ask questions/seek clarification on the implications of the need for students to experience the concepts for their work.

How will they set about ensuring that students relate the material presented in the programme to their own experience?

Ask for feedback.

### SLIDE 19

**A Three-stage Cyclical Process**

Teaching the programme involves a three-stage cyclical process (adapted from Morris 2009):

1. awareness
2. intervention and action
3. evaluation and reflection.

## Facilitator's notes

The process of teaching the programme starts with awareness or noticing. This involves asking the students to notice how the character strengths that are introduced in the programme actually show up in the world around them, including in other people. As Ian Morris (2009) writes, 'noticing is a skill that has to be learned and arises from stillness and patience.' A central skill that the programme teaches is the importance of noticing things about ourselves and others.

The second stage is the intervention. Students are provided with opportunities for discussion and activity sheets which involve them in reflecting upon their own experiences and learning about the practical ways that they can engage with the character strengths being taught.

The third stage involves evaluation and reflection. The students should be encouraged to get into the habit of tuning in to the effects of the discussion and activities that they have engaged with and reflecting on how useful these have been for them. Students must be encouraged to reflect meaningfully on the effectiveness both of the components that make up the session and on the session as a whole.

## Activity

Provide an opportunity for participants to ask questions/seek clarification on the stages of delivering the programme.

**SLIDE 20**

**Concluding the Programme**

- Optimism, flow and happy memories are essential to happiness (Seligman 2003).
- Emotional memories depend upon how an experience concludes (Fredrickson 2009).

## Facilitator's notes

Explain to participants that it is important to conclude the programme with a focus on 'what has gone well'. Positive endings, termed 'peak end rule' by positive psychologists, create overall positive memories of an activity or event, and thus ensuring that the programme ends on a high note will help to make difficulties disappear when students reflect back on the programme.

## Activity

Ask participants to consider what strategies they can use to ensure that each session and also the programme as a whole ends on a positive note.

Ask participants for feedback and note down suggestions.

# GENERAL GUIDANCE ON DELIVERING THE PROGRAMME

The programme that forms the backbone of this book is a 'stand-alone' resource. However, it is important that its principles and approaches are incorporated into the general school routine. Ian Morris (2009, p.6), head of Well-being at Wellington College in Berkshire, explains why this is the case when he writes, 'teaching well-being is in many ways like teaching of other subjects with one important difference. The subject is *directly* about the students and about being human, rather than about ideas.'

## Teaching well-being

Teaching well-being (and in this context I am using this term as a generic term to include the teaching of the character strengths which is the focus of the programme presented in this resource) is therefore not quite like other academic disciplines as it relates directly to experiences that students have in their daily lives – therefore to teach *about* well-being would be to miss the point. The teaching of well-being must have *experience* as its main aim. We should be teaching students how to *do* well-being – that is, experience and practise the concepts in everyday life. The aim of the subject is to allow students to experience something that can then be put into action in their own lives.

The guiding principle for delivering the programme is therefore that students should first experience the ideas for themselves and then reflect and evaluate their relevance and usefulness for their own lives. It is generally becoming accepted that schools have a vital role to play in enabling children and young people to lead happy lives. However, if schools are genuinely committed to putting happiness and well-being at the heart of their ethos and activities it is essential that they recognise that teaching well-being is not like the teaching of other subjects, and experience and student participation is a vital strategy for its success. Positive psychologists, Keyes and Lopez (2002) capture this concept when they explain that 'views of clients as "passive receptacles" have become antiquated' which highlights the essential need to incorporate a child's or adult's active participation in his or her own growth.'

Ian Morris (2009) explains that teaching well-being involves a three-stage process:

1. awareness and noticing

2. intervention and action

3. evaluation and reflection.

## Stage 1: Awareness and noticing

This initial stage takes place when the students are introduced to the character strengths which form the backbone of the programme. Noticing is a primary skill in well-being because it is the alert system which tells us that things are going well or things are not going well and when we need to make changes in our lives. For example, positive psychologists suggest that using our signature strengths, which are the focus of this resource, is accompanied by feelings of ownership, authenticity and joyful, enthusiastic feelings such as, 'This is the real me.'

It will be important to encourage students to be aware of their reactions to the material being presented in the sessions and the feelings that accompany the recognition of using their signature strengths. Noticing and awareness arise from stillness and paying attention and these are skills which may have to be learnt. The practice of mindfulness, which is described on pp.36–7 of this resource, is a helpful tool for introducing calming, quieting practices into the classroom that will improve mood and assist learning. An important aspect of the programme will involve teaching students to become aware of changes in the mind or body that are brought on by their positive or negative states.

## Stage 2: Intervention and action

The interventions and activities that comprise the programme are presented in 24 sessions. Each session describes a character strength. The sessions are presented in six sections, each section representing one of the six virtues. It is essential that the programme is delivered flexibly according to the needs of the students. The programme is not necessarily intended to be taught as a whole in linear order. Facilitators may therefore wish, as a starting point, to select one of the six sections to present to students. Less is more; it is more important for effective learning to take place rather than the facilitator to feel under pressure to deliver the whole programme or more sessions than there is time for in real terms.

The facilitator should consider at the planning stage the needs of the students and the time available to deliver the programme. A useful starting point might be for the practitioner to consider which of the strengths have most relevance to the students and deliver those sessions. This could be as few as three or four sessions if that is what the facilitator considers will meet the needs of the particular group. The programme can be delivered to whole classes, small groups or to individual students as part of a mentoring, coaching or counselling session. Flexibility is the rule as to how the programme should be delivered and at all times the needs of the students must be paramount if they are to benefit from the programme.

## TIMING OF THE SESSIONS

It is anticipated that each session will last for approximately 45 minutes and this timing should include plenty of time for group discussion, partner work or individual work. The key criterion is that that students should feel that they 'own' and relate to the content of the sessions and are able to complete the activities thoughtfully based on their own experience. The aim of each session is for each student to experience and learn how to relate to the strength being taught in real terms so that they can then:

- experience it
- put it into practice in their own lives
- reflect upon its usefulness in their lives.

## ACTIVITY SHEETS

The activity sheets which accompany each session are intended to be used as starting points to activate students' active involvement in the material being presented and spark off responses based on their individual experiences and feelings. As Ian Morris (2009) explains:

> just reading a worksheet on the benefits of altruism will have little effect: getting the students to practise a random act of kindness and write about the effect it had will raise their chances of using that skill more frequently. (Morris 2009, p.7)

The imperative of creating opportunities for the students to practise and experiment with the strengths that are presented in the sessions cannot be overstated. Unless students have opportunities to relate to the concept being introduced in real terms and consider how it can affect them as individuals, effective learning will not take place. Students may have an intellectual grasp of the programme's content but it will not be, in Ian Morris's words, 'embedded in the core of their being'.

The programme therefore allows for a very flexible approach to delivery regarding time allocation and the order in which the sessions are delivered. Fit for purpose is the order of the day. The bottom line is that practitioners should have the confidence and flexibility to be able to deliver the programme in line with the needs of the students they are working with. This in our experience may mean repeating a session or leaving out the activities to enable useful class discussion or partner work to continue. This flexible approach has important implications for the choice of the facilitator. The facilitator must be committed to delivering the programme and also:

- feel comfortable with the subject area
- be able to easily and successfully engage with young people
- be emotionally stable
- have a working knowledge of positive psychology and the concepts and strategies that form the programme
- feel comfortable facilitating discussions on controversial subjects and provide good models of listening to differing viewpoints without necessarily agreeing with them
- have a commitment to building a 'strengths-based approach'.

## CREATING A CLIMATE WHERE POSITIVE CHANGE CAN OCCUR

In this section two approaches to developing a climate where positive change can occur are presented. These are motivational interviewing and a solution-focused approach. They are intended to support the facilitator with techniques and practical strategies to use for building student engagement and an interactive approach.

### Motivational interviewing

Motivational interviewing (MI) is a collaborative, person-centred form of guiding to elicit and strengthen motivation for change (Miller and Rollnick 2002). It is not a technique, trick or something that is done to individuals to make them change, rather it is a positive style of communicating with others about their difficulties with change and the possibilities of engaging in healthier behaviours that are in accord with the individual's strengths and goals. It has been defined as a person-centred method of enhancing motivation to change by exploring and resolving ambivalence.

The central premise of this approach is that individuals are not always ready to change their behaviours and so there is no assumption that they will do so. Successful behaviour change is dependent upon enhancing the individual's motivation.

MI is a helpful strategy to use with young people because it takes into account the possibility of the young person's ambivalence about change. Ambivalence in the context of MI is described as the uncomfortable feeling that individuals have when they are unsure whether they want to change. The process of MI effectively puts individuals in touch with their ambivalence and enables them to work it through so that they are motivated to make changes for themselves. Individuals learn that change is an uncomfortable process and their ambivalence is usually an inevitable stage in the process of change.

Enabling young people to understand the stages of change is part of the process of increasing their intrinsic motivation to alter their behaviour. MI teaches that resolution does not happen all at once There are six recognised stages in the change process. They are:

1. pre-thinking
2. thinking
3. preparation and deciding
4. action and doing
5. maintenance
6. termination – at this end stage the desired behaviour has become an integral part of the individual's identity.

Although in theory the six stages are clearly identified, in practice individuals rarely move smoothly and consistently from one stage to the next. Relapsing remains the rule rather than the exception when it comes to change. Most individuals slip up at some point, returning to the thinking or even the pre-thinking stage before renewing their efforts. The feelings triggered by relapsing can be uncomfortable and individuals are typically embarrassed, ashamed and guilty. They may also feel that their efforts have been wasted and demoralisation may set in. Relapsing therefore must be viewed as an important part of the change process and setbacks should not be regarded as failure or reason to give up but as an opportunity to learn from and as a trigger for renewed emphasis on the importance of moving one's life positively forward.

Familiarising young people with the stages of change will help to ensure that they work through the process in a systematic way by stating the desired behaviour or goal and identifying short-term goals, long-term goals and action points for themselves. The framework of MI can be summarised as follows:

1. Reflect on a behaviour that you want to change and identify a personal goal. Ensure that there are SMART (specific, measurable, achievable, realistic and time-bound) criteria for this goal.

2. Think about what is it that you want to do differently.

3. Identify your long-term goal – consider what would be different in your life, and if and how you will know that things are better for you and others around you.

4. Identify your short-term goal. This must be achievable within thirty days. Consider the following:

   – What would be different over the next few days and weeks if you make the change?

   – What will you be doing differently in the short term if you make this change?

   – Identify the greatest barrier to change.

5. Action steps – write down a list of action steps that need to be achieved in order to meet this short-term goal and set a date to review this with someone who you trust and has your best interests at heart.

## Solution-focused approach

A solution-focused approach introduces the idea of possibilities leading to positive change. Its techniques are easily learned and safe to practise. Solution-focused approaches enable practitioners to become effective helpers as the strategies that are used in this approach are designed to encourage individuals to explore their strengths and resources rather than concentrating on their problems and deficits. This approach takes for granted that students are the experts in their own lives and learning and that the task of facilitators is to ask appropriate questions, assist progress and enable individuals to:

- identify what their goals or preferred future will look like
- notice things in their lives that are going well or parts of their goals that are already happening.

Underlying any kind of solution-focused work is the positive and respectful attitude to those we are working with. We therefore assume that students want to do well, have or can develop goals and have the capacity and personal resources to move towards them.

## PROBLEM-FREE TALK

A solution-focused approach has a great deal in common with appreciative enquiry, which is described on p.37 of this resource. It involves talking to the individual about what is going well in their life and thus enables the listener to identify the young person's potential, strengths, resources and successes, places a focus on the things that are going well and also demonstrates an active interest in the student.

## GOALS/PREFERRED FUTURE

Use of the 'miracle question' technique, 'If everything was going well for you what would your life look like?' can help a young person to identify clear goals and build a clear description of their preferred future. This process can be extremely motivating.

It is important to ensure that the young person describes their goals and preferred future in detail. A useful question is, 'What else?' Well-described goals will be:

- positive
- broken down into small, achievable steps
- specific and observable
- realistic.

The facilitator should use questions that imply a positive outcome:

- *How* will you do that?
- *When* will this happen?
- *What* will you be doing?
- *What* will be happening?

Avoiding 'problem talk' and enabling students to focus on times when things are going well can help reduce the possibility of them being overwhelmed by the challenge and helps to emphasise the positive things that they are already doing.

## SCALING QUESTIONS

Scaling questions are tools that are used to identify useful differences for the student and may also help to identify goals. The extent of the scale typically ranges from 'the worst things could be' (1) to 'the best things could be' (10). Students are asked to rate their current position on the scale. 'On a scale of 1–10 how well do you think you are doing?' can help students express themselves and can bypass a paucity of vocabulary; when words fail, numbers can come to the rescue. Further questions are then used to help the student to:

- identify their resources: 'What's stopping you from slipping one point lower down the scale?'
- exceptions: 'On a day when you are one point higher on the scale what would tell you it was a "one point higher day"?'
- describe a preferred future: 'Where on the scale would be good enough and what would that day look like?'

## DELIVERING THE SESSIONS

### Length of sessions

A time allocation of 45 minutes is suggested for each session. However, as discussed above, this may be extended (time permitting) or reduced according to the size of the group. In our experience of delivering the programme the larger the group the longer the session is likely to take in order to ensure that the session is interactive and that there are plenty of opportunities for discussion involving all students.

### Structure of the sessions

Each session apart from the first follows a similar structure. However, it is important to emphasise that this is a suggested arrangement and the facilitators should feel free to adapt this structure according to the needs of the individual group of students:

- Preparation: the relevant activity sheets should be available at the start of the session. Key words and aims of the session should be visible on the board.
- Review of previous session.
- Introduction to the session.
- Class discussion.
- Activity.
- Review of activity.
- Final plenary.

## *Stage 3: Evaluation and reflection*

The third and final stage in the process of teaching well-being is evaluation and reflection. This process should not be simply left to the end of the programme but should be an integral part of every session. Students should be encouraged to get into the habit of questioning the ideas that they are being presented with throughout the programme and also be prepared to debate the usefulness of the activities. Students must be enabled to be open about aspects of the session that may not work for them and be encouraged to reflect on what could have been done differently and be able to suggest solutions. The solution-focused approach and motivational interviewing described in the previous section will enable the facilitator to address the students' concerns positively and constructively. A key success criterion for the programme is that students should be able to reflect meaningfully on the effectiveness of the sessions and on the programme as a whole.

## MEASURING IMPACT

As noted above, the aim of the programme is not to teach students facts but to enable them to become active participants in their own growth. This involves enabling students to:

- be able to identify their signature strengths
- claim them as strong points

- name them
- share them with others
- actively use their strengths whenever possible
- discover new ways of using them.

The impact of the programme can also be measured by whether the facilitator considers that as a result of the programme students:

- notice things about themselves and the world around them and are aware of their internal alert system that lets them know when things are going well or not going well for them
- know the practical things and actions that they need to take to keep themselves happy and healthy
- report increased satisfaction from positive activities which involve using their signature strengths.

As a result of the programme students should be able to have the following internal dialogue (adapted from Morris 2009):

- I know when something helpful/unhelpful is happening in my life. I know this because…
- When…is happening in my life, I know that I have to do…
- I know this is successful because…

## Team approach

We would suggest if possible trialling the programme with two facilitators involved who will not only support each other but can provide continuity in case of absence.

There should also be a member of the senior leadership team who will support the facilitators. In our experience of delivering the programme in schools, facilitators may sometimes experience a personal involvement with the programme which might cause distress. If this should occur then supervision should be available to the individual.

Students may ask for information outside the facilitators' experience or knowledge base. A list of useful sources of information and relevant websites is provided at the end of this resource.

## Informing parents/carers

It might be appropriate to send an information sheet or letter to parents/carers so that they are aware of the content of the programme.

## Support system

We have already mentioned the need for support for the facilitators but consideration should also be given to the needs of the young people as the programme may bring up issues that they may want to explore in more depth. Most schools and settings have a support structure for students and at the start of the programme young people should be reminded that they should make an opportunity to speak to the facilitator or another adult in the school if they have concerns.

Supportline is both a website and a helpline which offers confidential emotional support for children, young adults and adults. It is a useful point of contact as it identifies local and national bodies, and also organisations which will offer help and support to young people. See www.supportline.org.uk, or the helpline 01708 765200.

## Confidentiality

As the programme is directly about the students and about being human, some of the sessions will inevitably raise sensitive issues and students may feel vulnerable sharing aspects of their lives. It is therefore important that confidentiality is emphasised and established at the beginning of the programme and reinforced throughout the sessions. The general rule is that contributions made in the sessions should stay in the room. All must be aware and understand that if something is raised which indicates that the young person may be at risk then the facilitator is obliged to report these concerns.

## Child protection

If the facilitator has any concerns regarding the safety of a young person these concerns should be discussed with a senior member of staff and local safeguarding procedures should be adhered to.

# REFERENCES

American Psychiatric Association (2000) *Diagnostic and Statistical Manual of Mental Disorders (Fourth Edition, Text Revision)*. Washington, DC: APA.

Aristotle (350 BC) *Nicomachean Ethics*. See Ross, W.D. (ed.) Oxford (1931) Available at http://classics.mit.edu/Aristotle/nicomachaen.8.viii.html, accessed on 5 January 2012.

Asthana, A. (2004) 'I want to be Beyoncé.' *The Observer*, 1 December 2004.

Barnes, J. (ed.) (1984) *The Complete Works of Aristotle*, Vols 1–2. Princeton, NJ: Princeton University Press.

Ben-Shahar, T. (2007) *Happier: Learn the Secrets to Daily Joy and Lasting Fulfilment*. New York: McGraw-Hill.

Boniwell, I. (2006) *Positive Psychology in a Nutshell*. London: Personal Well-Being Centre.

Brown, B. (2010) *The Gifts of Imperfection: Let Go of Who You Think You're Supposed to Be and Embrace Who You Are*. Center City, MN: Hazelden.

Buckingham, M. and Clifton, D. (2005) *Now Discover Your Strengths: How to Develop Your Strengths and Those of the People You Manage*. London: Pocket Books.

Clifton, D.O. and Anderson, C.E. (2002) *StrengthsQuest: Discover and develop your strengths in academics, career and beyond*. Washington, D.C.: The Gallup Organization.

Cooperrider, D.L. (2001) *Lessons from the Field: Applying Appreciative Inquiry*. New York: Thin Book Publishing.

Craig, C. (2007) *Creating Confidence: A Handbook for Professionals Working with Young People*. Glasgow: The Centre for Confidence and Wellbeing.

Csikszentmihalyi, M. (1990) *Flow: The Psychology of Optimal Experience*. New York: HarperCollins.

Diener, E. and Seligman, M.E. (2002) 'Very happy people.' *Psychological Science 13*, 1, 81–84.

Ellis, A. (1962) *Reason and Emotion in Psychotherapy*. New York: Lyle Stuart.

Emmons, R.A. (2007) *Thanks: How the New Science of Gratitude Can Make You Happier*. New York: Houghton Mifflin.

Erikson, E. (1963) *Childhood and Society*. New York: Norton.

Fox Eades, J. (2008) *Celebrating Strengths: Building Strengths-based Schools*. Coventry: CAPP Press.

Fredrickson, B. (2009) *Positivity*. New York: Crown Publishers.

Gable, S.L., Reis, H.T., Impett, E. and Asher, E.R. (2004) 'What do you do when things go right? The intrapersonal and interpersonal benefits of sharing positive events.' *Journal of Personality and Social Psychology 87*, 228–245.

Gilbert, D. (2007) *Stumbling on Happiness*. London: HarperCollins.

Gladwell, M. (2009) *Outliers: The Story of Success*. London: Penguin Books.

Hodges, T. and Clifton, D. (2004) 'Strengths-Based Development in Practice.' In A. Linley and S. Joseph (eds) *Positive Psychology in Practice*. New York: Wiley.

Huppert, F. (2007) 'Learning about happiness.' *1st European Conference on Happiness and its Causes.* Conference Workbook, 13–14 October, London.

James, O. (2007) *Affluenza.* London: Vermilion.

Keyes, C.L.M. and Lopez, S.J. (2002) 'Towards a Science of Mental Health: Positive Directions in Diagnosis and Interventions'. In Snyder, C.R. and Lopez, S.J. (eds) *Handbook of Positive Psychology.* New York: Oxford University Press.

Linley, A. (2008) *Average to A+.* Coventry: CAPP Press.

Linley, A., Willars, J., and Biswas-Diener, R. (2010) *The Strengths Book.* Coventry: CAPP Press.

Lyubomirsky, S. (2007) *The How of Happiness: A Scientific Approach to Getting the Life You Want.* New York: Penguin.

MacConville, R.M. (2009) *Teaching Happiness: A Ten Step Curriculum for Creating Positive Classrooms.* Teach to Inspire Series. London: Optimus Education.

MacLean, K.L. (2004) *Peaceful Piggy Meditation.* Park Ridge, IL: Albert Whitman and Co.

Maslow, A. (1971) *The Farther Reaches of Human Nature.* New York: Viking.

Miller, R.M. and Rollnick, S. (2002) *Motivational Interviewing: Preparing Young People for Change.* New York: The Guildford Press

Morris, I. (2009) *Teaching Happiness and Well-being in Schools.* London: Continuum Books.

Nettle, D. (2005) *Happiness: The Science Behind Your Smile.* Oxford: Open University Press.

Palmer, S. (2006) *Toxic Childhood: How the Modern World is Damaging Our Children and What We Can Do About It.* London: Orion Books.

Peterson, C. (2006) *A Primer in Positive Psychology.* New York: Oxford University Press.

Peterson, C. and Seligman, M. (2004) *Character Strengths and Virtues: A Classification and Handbook.* Washington, DC: American Psychological Association.

Rath, T. (2007) *Strengths Finder.* New York: Gallup Press.

Seligman, M. (2003) *Authentic Happiness: Using the New Positive Psychology to Realize Your Potential for Lasting Fulfilment.* New York: Free Press.

Seligman, M. (2006) *Learned Optimism: How to Change Your Mind and Your Life.* New York: Vintage Books.

Seligman, M. (2011) *Flourish: A New Understanding of Happiness and Well-Being and How to Achieve Them.* London: Nicholas Brearley Publishing.

Seligman, M. and Csikszentmihalyi, M. (2000) 'Positive Psychology: An introduction.' *American Psychologist 55,* 5–14.

Seligman, M., Reivich, K., Jaycox, L. and Gillham, J. (1995) *The Optimistic Child.* New York: Houghton Mifflin.

Smith, A. (1759) *The Theory of Moral Sentiments,* Raphael, D., and MacFie, A. (eds) (1976). Oxford: Oxford University Press.

Snyder, C.R. and Lopez, S.J. (eds) (2002) *Handbook of Positive Psychology.* New York: Oxford University Press.

Staniforth, M. (1964) *The Complete Text of Marcus Aurelius' Meditations.* London: Penguin Books.

Sternberg, R.J. (1998) 'A balance of theory and wisdom.' *Review of General Psychology 2,* 347–365.

Ungar, M. (2006) *Strengths-Based Counselling with At-risk Youth.* Thousand Oaks, CA: Corwin Press.

Valliant, G.E. (1977) *Adaptation to Life.* Boston, MA: Little, Brown.

# DELIVERING THE PROGRAMME

# WISDOM AND KNOWLEDGE

## COGNITIVE STRENGTHS THAT ENTAIL THE ACQUISITION AND USE OF KNOWLEDGE

# Chapter 1

# CREATIVITY

## THINKING OF NOVEL AND PRODUCTIVE WAYS TO DO THINGS

## Introduction

In this chapter the students are introduced to the topic of 'creativity'. This involves thinking about the notion of creativity and how to be productive in attempting new challenges and engaging in new areas of knowledge and learning. Students are introduced to the concept of setting themselves appropriate challenges by identifying the things that they can do and then building upon these in order to further identify future targets and possibilities. There is also a focus upon the need to change certain behaviours, identifying those that they engage in that are currently not productive and positive and the ways in which they can move forward in order to change their behaviours and achieve better outcomes for themselves.

There is an opportunity to also consider the goal setting process, formulating stepped plans which ensure alternative options so as to make real differences in their lives. The idea here is to also reinforce the fact that sometimes things don't go to plan and that we need to identify what we can do when situations do not turn out as expected. The state of productivity can often be achieved by ensuring that we avoid catastrophising situations. It is very easy to catastrophise when we feel tired or less positive and it is important for students to develop self-reflection skills in order to avoid such negative cycles and patterns of behaviour.

### ACTIVITY 1

#### A New Challenge

Students can initially be presented with the new challenge activity sheet. In this activity they are asked to consider first the things that they can do – this is really important in terms of reinforcing self-esteem and identifying current levels of skills, abilities and areas of knowledge. They next are asked to consider what they want to do in the future – these may be short-term or long-term goals. The next part of the activity involves identifying things that they really want to do – this is a distinction that needs to be clarified at the outset. These are things that the student may really wish to engage in or change about themselves, that might make a very big difference to them in the current situation and in their future lives. Finally, they are asked to identify things that they really, really want to do. These are their ultimate goals, things for the future that they may wish or dream about at this current point in time.

Students are then asked to identify one of these things and to also clarify why this might be a challenge. This is important because very often we can be tempted into visualising the most extraordinary and unachievable goals and then become negative and disenchanted with the process when we feel that we can't achieve them. Identifying why a certain task might be a challenge is very important because this then allows us to work out the steps that we need to take in order to achieve that specific goal.

## ACTIVITY 2

### Changing Behaviours

In this activity the students are asked to consider things that they do that are currently productive and positive. This could involve patterns of learning, ways of learning, ways of keeping fit, ways of making and maintaining positive relationships. The next step in this process is to consider what they could do in order to be more productive in each of these situations and to finally identify changes they could make in their behaviour to achieve a better outcome. It may be useful for the facilitator to provide an example as follows:

- Things that I do that are currently productive and positive – I currently go to the gym twice a week in order to keep fit and make myself feel good about myself.

- Ways I could be more productive in each situation – I could probably talk to a trainer in the gym in order to refine my current programme. It may be also useful to consider ways that I could slot in further times in which to keep fit during each week.

- Changes I could make in my behaviour to achieve a better outcome:
  1. Timetabling in an additional slot.
  2. Arrange to meet with the trainer.
  3. Produce and engage in a plan with the trainer in order to make myself even fitter for the future.

## ACTIVITY 3

### New Goals

In this activity the students are asked to identify a new goal for themselves, something that they really wish that they could achieve in the future. They are then asked to proceed in making a stepped plan in order to achieve this goal, identifying four specific steps with alternatives from steps 2–4, that is, this is what I could do if this was not an appropriate step at this stage. What is also important here is that students are asked to identify rewards that they will give themselves at each step in the process. This is particularly important – in order to keep positive and keep motivated we need to have rewards, and we need also not to feel guilty about rewarding ourselves for when we do things well.

## ACTIVITY 4

### Staying Productive – Avoid Blowing Up!

Sometimes when we do feel tired or less positive it can be more difficult to stay productive, positive and motivated. If we encounter a small problem we can often be tempted to blow this up out of all proportion and make things worse than they really are. The students are provided with an example of this on the activity sheet. Students are then asked to test their own thoughts, finding the evidence for why they have blown something out of proportion. It will be important to identify and consider a time when they have done this, for example when they didn't do particularly well on a test and then blamed themselves entirely for what had occurred, or when a relationship had gone sour and they blamed themselves for the fact that this had happened. The students are asked to examine this situation, identify the evidence for the way that they felt, reflect further upon this and then check it out with others. Checking it out with others is very important, as sometimes the way that we perceive things can be very different to the way that others do. For example, if I ask a friend to confirm my own viewpoint that I was outrageously badly behaved in a certain situation, I might find that they have a different perception that is more positive. This is because, unlike me, they have not blown this out of proportion.

## Plenary

The students can finally focus upon the following questions as part of the plenary discussion:

- What have we learnt about the way in which we creatively think about ourselves and our behaviours?
- What prompts us to be more productive?
- What holds us back from being more productive?
- Why is it important not to blow things out of proportion?
- Does everyone find it easy to be creative and maintain a positive outlook on life?
- How has this session been useful in terms of identifying future aspirations and goals?
- What else would have made this session more helpful? Share ideas.

## A New Challenge

Pick one thing that you really, really want to do and identify why this may be a 'challenge' for you.

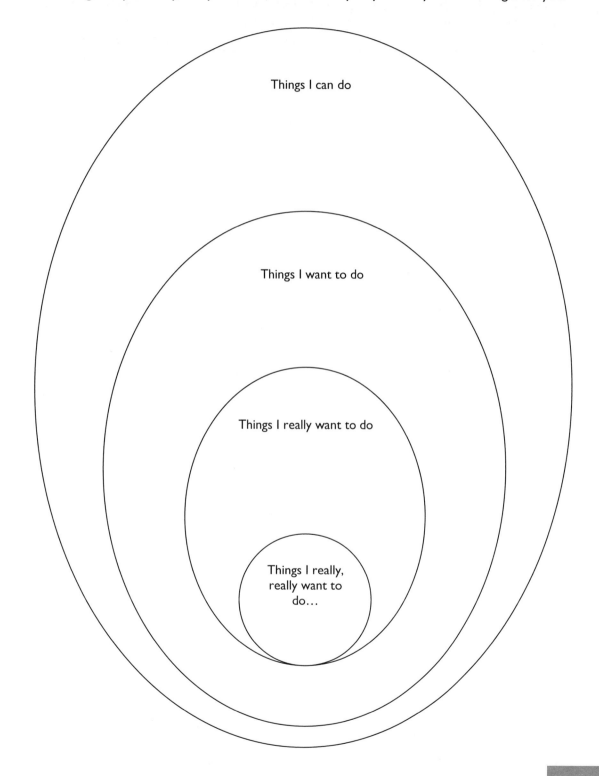

Things I can do

Things I want to do

Things I really want to do

Things I really, really want to do…

## Changing Behaviours

| Things I do that are productive and positive | Ways I could be more productive in each situation | Changes I could make in my behaviour to achieve a better outcome |
|---|---|---|
| | | |
| | | |
| | | |
| | | |

# New Goals

My new goal is to:

This is my PLAN to
achieve this goal

If I get it wrong or things
don't work out I can try
something else

These are the rewards I
will give myself as I work
towards my goal

| Step 1 | | Reward 1 |

| Step 2 | Alternative | Reward 2 |

| Step 3 | Alternative | Reward 3 |

| Step 4 | Alternative | Reward 4 |

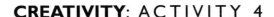

# CREATIVITY: ACTIVITY 4

## Staying Productive – Avoid Blowing Up!

Sometimes when we feel tired or less positive it can be more difficult to stay productive. If we encounter a small problem we can be tempted to 'blow it up' and make things worse than they are.

> I got the answer wrong – everyone laughed. They ALL think I'm stupid! I'll never try again.

> I only got 72% and not 100% – it's not good enough.

Ever said it?

To stay productive we need to STOP, THINK and REFLECT! Test your thoughts by <u>finding the evidence</u>. Use the four steps:

1. Examine it!
2. Look for the evidence.
3. Stop, think and reflect.
4. Check it out with others.

# Chapter 2

# CURIOSITY

## TAKING AN INTEREST IN ALL OF ONGOING EXPERIENCE

## Introduction

In this chapter the students are introduced to the notion of maintaining and taking an interest in what is going on in their lives and in the lives of others. This is particularly important in terms of maintaining a positive outlook and maintaining motivation in all areas of our lives. The students are asked to consider times when they have engaged in negative automatic thinking and to then begin the process of reframing some of these negative thoughts. This is a hugely useful life skill which will ensure the maintenance of well-being in the future.

Identifying their interests also helps to reinforce the fact that they are individuals and unique. They may share their interests with others but even if this is not the case it is important to reinforce the fact that these interests and passions make them who they are and that they are important in themselves. Students are also introduced to the concept of learning from experience, identifying how when things go wrong they can still learn from these situations.

### ACTIVITY 1

### What is Happening to Me?

In this activity the students are asked to consider and identify their current ongoing experiences. What is it that is happening to them in the world at this current point in time? What is happening to their friends and family, the people who help and support them and also what is happening in their country and the world as a whole? This is vital! None of us can live in a social vacuum. We are all social beings and have the opportunity to take an interest in what is going on in our own lives and in those of others and the world at large.

Identifying these factors helps us to realise the way in which the social context frames both our own personalities and experience and also gives us the opportunity to reflect and learn from others, and think about what is going on in the world around us. There is also the notion of empathy here in that students are required to think about what is happening to others who help and support them. It may be useful to further consider the ways in which their own behaviours impact upon these people and whether or not there are any things that they can do differently in order to maintain and further develop more positive relationships.

## ACTIVITY 2

### Being Positive

This is a particularly important element to the session. We all need to feel positive about ourselves if we want to take an interest in others. Sometimes this means that we have to catch negative thoughts and reframe them at the outset. This is important because negative thinking can, very often, not only affect our own self-esteem but also prevent us from developing and maintaining positive relationships with others.

Students are asked to identify negative automatic thoughts that they often have – ideas that pop into our heads and make us feel down. For example, I'm fat, I'm ugly, I'm stupid, I'm rubbish at doing this. Students can be prompted to identify four such thoughts that they themselves have had and then to engage in a reframing exercise. How can they turn these negatives into more positive statements which will then allow them to move on and build more positive outcomes for themselves?

## ACTIVITY 3

### My Interests

In this activity the students are asked to thought-storm, recording their interests on the format provided – this can be either in written or visual form. The idea here is to reinforce the interests that they have and the ways in which these make them the person that they are. There is also an element of identifying how these interests show others who they are and the positive outcomes that they've gained from engaging in certain activities.

## ACTIVITY 4

### Learning From Experience

Sometimes things in our lives don't always go right and we experience and encounter situations that cause us problems or setbacks. Students are asked to engage in an A, B, C process, identifying a) adversity – something that happened to them that is negative, b) belief – what did they think about this and why did it happen? and c) consequences – what did they feel and what did they and others do about this situation? This process allows them to focus on the fact that even when things go wrong it is important to learn from those experiences.

Encountering adversity and setbacks does not mean that we have to cave in and fall into a negative cycle or pattern of behaviour. Very often when something goes wrong it is possible by being reflective and analysing the situation further to identify what it was that actually went wrong and what could be done differently in a similar situation in the future. This is vital if we are to maintain a positive outlook on life.

## Plenary

The students can finally focus upon the following questions as part of the plenary discussion:

- What have we learnt about our own experiences?
- Why is it important to recognise what is happening to us in our lives and in our social and world contexts?

- How can we maintain a positive outlook on life?
- Is the reframing strategy useful?
- Is it always possible to learn from experience and mistakes?
- Why is this a useful strategy to use and further develop?
- Has this session been useful?
- What else would have made this session more helpful? Share ideas.

## What is Happening to Me?

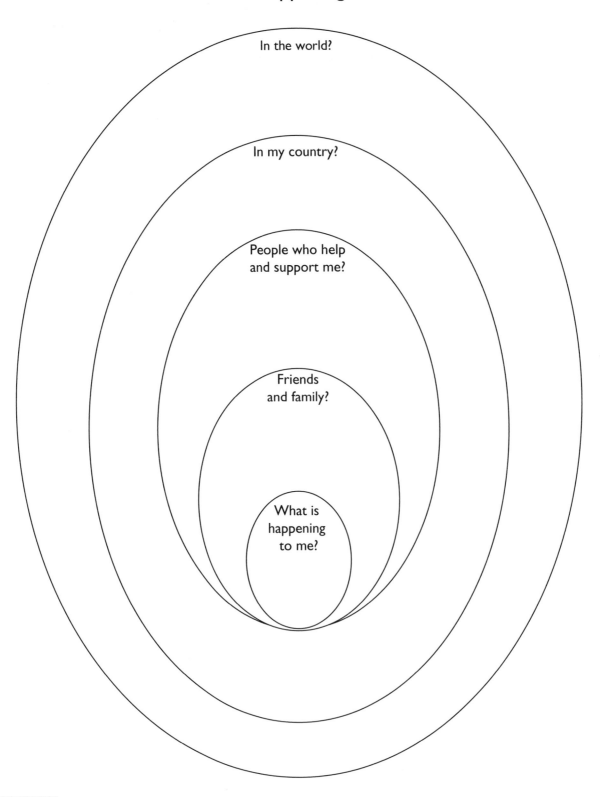

In the world?

In my country?

People who help
and support me?

Friends
and family?

What is
happening
to me?

## Being Positive

We have to feel positive about ourselves if we want to take an interest in others and the world around us. Sometimes this means that we need to catch those negative thoughts and REFRAME them! Have a go for yourself!

| Negative Automatic Thought (NAT) | Reframe! |
|---|---|
| *Example:* I am really rubbish at doing exams! I know I'll fail! | I find exams difficult but I know that I can get some help with study and revision skills so I have more chance of passing. |
|  |  |
|  |  |
|  |  |

## My Interests

Use the thought-storming format to record your interests!

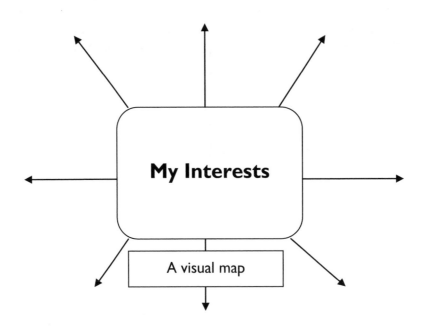

A visual map

## Key focus questions

To what extent do your interests show others 'who' you are?

What really positive experiences have your interests given you and what have you learnt from these?

# CURIOSITY: ACTIVITY 4

## Learning From Experience

Sometimes things don't always go 'right' and we have some situations that cause us a problem or setback. Pick your own situation – think of a time you learnt from experience – and record your own 'ABC' in the chart below.

| **A**<br>**Adversity**<br>Something happens. | What happened? |
|---|---|
| **B**<br>**Belief**<br>What did I think about it? Why did this happen? | Your thoughts/beliefs |
| **C**<br>**Consequences**<br>How did I feel and what did I and others do? | The consequences |

Finally, what did you learn from this experience?

What could you think, feel and do differently next time something like this happens in order to achieve a better outcome?

# Chapter 3

# OPENMINDEDNESS

## THINKING THINGS THROUGH AND EXAMINING THEM FROM ALL SIDES

## Introduction

In this chapter students are introduced to the notion of alternative viewpoints and the importance and need to understand and respect the perspectives of others. They are asked to initially identify their own viewpoints in a range of areas such as what they think about politics, role models, religion, being successful. This provides an opportunity to consider how their views might be different to those of others. There is also focus upon the importance of always looking at both sides to any situation or story. Are things black and white or are there advantages and disadvantages to most situations?

It is also important for students to be able to continually reflect upon and evaluate their own patterns of thinking. Sometimes we can close our minds to certain options or situations because we have preconceived ideas or have stereotyped certain people or situations in some way. It is therefore important to identify the evidence for and against the way that we think in order to avoid thinking mistakes. The notion of empathy is also clearly very important in this chapter. It is very important in our lives that we can see things from others' perspectives and put ourselves in their shoes in order to maintain positive relationships and also to truly understand and engage in respectful relationships with others.

### ACTIVITY 1

#### My Viewpoint

In this activity the students are asked to consider the ways in which they think about a range of different situations and topics. This can be done in discussion with the facilitator or in the group as appropriate; however, it is important for each individual to identify their own viewpoints as the idea here is to reinforce the fact that we have and maintain our own points of view on a range of topics and areas. What is important is then to consider how our views are different to those of others. For example, one person, for a range of reasons, may believe that the death penalty is a just and right option for certain people who have committed a serious crime whereas others may have a range of beliefs, particularly religious beliefs, that may prevent them from taking on this viewpoint. Once again, what is important is to reinforce the fact that we all have the right to be who we are and to hold our views. However, what is also important is that these views and belief systems do not negatively impact upon others.

## ACTIVITY 2

### Is It Black and White?

The students can refer to some of their own ideas and perceptions which were identified in the previous activity. For example, they may hold the position that celebrities are important to society. They then would have to identify the advantages to holding this view – what is it that makes this a positive and advantageous position to take? For example, celebrities may do a lot of good in terms of their charity work, they may also provide positive role images to young people in terms of appearance and behaviour. They can then identify the disadvantages. Once again this activity reinforces the fact that most positions that we hold, or views that we have in our lives, will have advantages and disadvantages and there may be very few without at least one disadvantage.

## ACTIVITY 3

### Seeing It Differently

In this activity the students are asked to examine their own thinking. The idea here is to present the notion of openmindedness and the importance of maintaining this kind of stance in the way that we think. This is important as the way we think clearly impacts upon the way we feel and the way that we behave. Students can identify a negative thought that they may have had about themselves, for example, I am fat and ugly. They can then identify the evidence for this thought and the evidence against it.

This kind of motivational interviewing technique/strategy is particularly useful in helping us to move on from negative thinking patterns. For example, if we can find evidence that proves our assumption wrong then this can help us to move on. In this particular example, a friend may say, 'Actually you're not that fat, you're slightly overweight and there is something that you can do about it.' It is important for students to identify when they are making thinking mistakes such as blowing things out of proportion, blaming themselves or forgetting their own strengths or predicting failure. These are key thinking mistakes that human beings can engage in which do not lend themselves to maintaining a positive outlook on life.

## ACTIVITY 4

### Being in Your Shoes

The students are encouraged to look at things from other perspectives. They are presented with a range of situations on situation cards. These could be photocopied prior to the start of the session and cut into small cards to support the discussion. Examples include: the tallest girl in the class, the only boy in the school who hates sport, an eight-year-old child whose parents are divorcing, someone who has just lost their job, a woman who has just been told she has terminal cancer. The students are asked to consider what they would think if they were in this person's shoes. How would they feel being who they are, and how might others feel about this person? The development of empathy is clearly a key skill in terms of developing and maintaining positive relationships with others and it is important that students understand this fact and begin to further develop their skills in this area.

## Plenary

The students can then finally focus upon the following questions as part of the plenary discussion:

- What do we understand about the concept of openmindedness?

- Why is it important for us to have an awareness of our own viewpoints and opinions?

- Are things always black and white or can we identify advantages and disadvantages to different situations?

- What does empathy mean?

- Why is it important to be able to understand the perspectives and feelings of others?

- Is it important to be able to analyse our own thinking? If so, why? If not, why not?

- What kinds of thinking mistakes do we need to avoid in our lives and why would this be a good idea?

- Has this session been useful?

- What else would have made this session more helpful? Share ideas.

# **OPENMINDEDNESS**: ACTIVITY 1

## My Viewpoint

Look at the topics recorded on the activity sheet. What do you think about these issues? Discuss and then record your views and ideas below.

Winning a fortune?

Celebrities?                                    The death penalty?

Politics?

> **My Viewpoint**
>
> What do I think about…?

Role models?

Global warming?                                              Religion?

Poverty?          Being successful?

Discuss each in turn!

Stop, think and reflect – who would share your views and who might have different views to you and why?

## Is It Black and White?

|  | Advantages | Disadvantages |
|---|---|---|
| Position 1 |  |  |
| Position 2 |  |  |
| Position 3 |  |  |

# OPENMINDEDNESS: ACTIVITY 3

## Seeing It Differently

Examine your thinking. Be openminded and TEST your thoughts!

Write a negative thought below:

> 

What is the evidence for this thought?

...........................................................................................................

...........................................................................................................

What is the evidence against this thought?

...........................................................................................................

...........................................................................................................

What would my best friend say if they heard my thought?

...........................................................................................................

...........................................................................................................

What would my teacher say if she/he heard my thought?

...........................................................................................................

...........................................................................................................

What would my parents/carers say if they heard my thought?

...........................................................................................................

...........................................................................................................

What would I say to my best friend if they heard this thought?

...........................................................................................................

...........................................................................................................

Am I making THINKING MISTAKES – for example, blowing it out of proportion, self-blaming, forgetting my strengths or predicting failure?

...........................................................................................................

...........................................................................................................

# OPENMINDEDNESS: ACTIVITY 4

## Being in Your Shoes

Looking at things from all sides, what would:

1. you feel to be in this person's shoes?

2. they feel being who they are?

3. others feel about this person?

| | |
|---|---|
| A blind person | The tallest girl in the class |
| The only black student in the school | The only boy in the school who hates sport |
| A soldier returning from war having had a leg amputated | A lottery winner |
| Someone who has just lost their job | An eight-year-old child whose parents are divorcing |
| A woman who has just been told she has terminal breast cancer | A 15-year-old girl who thinks she is a lesbian |

# Chapter 4

# LOVE OF LEARNING

## MASTERING NEW SKILLS, TOPICS AND BODIES OF KNOWLEDGE

## Introduction

In this chapter students are introduced to the topic of learning and the ways in which we can all promote a genuine love of learning within ourselves. The importance of mastering new skills and knowledge and the ways in which these can both enrich our lives and increase our levels of self-esteem and well-being are also emphasised. There is a focus upon how we learn and students have the opportunity to consider a range of statements and ideas from John Holt's (1967) book *How Children Learn*. They are asked to discuss these ideas prior to formulating their own lists of Learning Motivators.

Students are introduced to the concept of 'flow' – a state we achieve in some activities and one which really reinforces the notions of enjoyment and love of learning. When we simply 'love' what we are doing/learning we enter this state of flow in which we forget time and we are able to challenge ourselves to improve our skills and achieve mastery of a specific task/body of knowledge. The learning tasks do not stress us because we simply find them so enjoyable. Once students have identified their own personal flow activities, they are finally required to formulate an Action Plan, identifying personal goals and rewards for the future.

### ACTIVITY 1

### How Children Learn

Students can initially be presented with the following quotation from John Holt's (1967) book *How Children Learn*:

> The child is curious. He wants to make sense out of things, find out how things work, gain competence and control over himself and his environment, and do what he can see other people doing. He is open, perceptive and experimental. He does not shut himself off from the strange, complicated world around him, but tastes it, touches it, hefts it, bends it, breaks it. To find out how reality works, he works on it. He is bold. He is not afraid of making mistakes and he is patient. He can tolerate an extraordinary amount of uncertainty, confusion, ignorance and suspense… School is not a place that gives much time or opportunity or reward for this kind of thinking and learning.

They can then proceed to discuss this, perhaps making reference to the following prompt questions:

- Do you agree that children are naturally open, perceptive and experimental? Is this how they learn best?

- What might prevent this type of learning in a) the home and b) the school context?

- Why do you think that John Holt might feel that a school is not the best place for providing such opportunities for learning and for developing a love of learning?

Students can work together in pairs/smaller groups in order to focus upon these questions, prior to feeding their ideas and thoughts back to the group as a whole. The facilitator can highlight any similarities and differences in their responses.

## ACTIVITY 2

### John Holt's Key Principles

John Holt made a series of claims regarding how young children learn and was passionate that his ideas should be understood by those in the teaching and learning professions. He felt that if they truly understood and believed in these ideas then they would change how they themselves thought about the learning process and that schools would become more 'child friendly' places in which learning could become an exciting and much-loved experience for all.

The students are asked to consider seven of his key principles, identifying what children would and would not need (in practical terms) in the school context in order to have these needs met most effectively. It may be useful for the facilitator to provide an example at the outset, such as: 'Children need plentiful amounts of quiet time to think'.

They need:

- a quiet place to go and reflect when things are busy

- time to think about what they've been asked to do – particularly if they don't 'get it' first time

- help to think about something once it's done and identify what they think they've learnt, what was hard/easy/enjoyable/less enjoyable and how they might learn or do this particular task differently/better next time

- parents/carers and teachers who listen to them and give them time to think and say things without interrupting or rushing them

- parents/carers and teachers who encourage them to think and value their ideas and creativity.

They do not need:

- classrooms that are too busy and have no areas for quiet work and reflection

- to be rushed into completing an activity or task when they don't really understand it and need more time to think

- to be pushed onto the next task without having time to reflect upon what they've just learnt

- parents/carers and teachers who interrupt, don't listen and don't give them enough time to formulate their thoughts and responses

- parents/carers and teachers who don't allow thinking time and don't show that they value children's ideas and creativity.

## ACTIVITY 3

### My Learning Motivators

In this activity, the students can build upon learning undertaken in the previous one in which they will have identified some of the key demotivating factors for young people in the learning context. The central objective here is to focus and reflect upon their own motivators – what is it that makes it easier for them to learn? Are they more motivated by subjects/topics that they enjoy? Does being good at something increase motivation to further develop their skills? Do they find rewards motivating and, if so, are these in the form of material goods or emotional rewards such as spending time with friends? Are they more motivated when working with/for/alongside certain kinds of people?

It may be helpful to provide the students with some time to discuss these questions prior to completing their individual Learning Motivators sheets. Completing this activity should help to clarify key motivators and the ways in which these might be used even more effectively in order to promote learning and achievement.

## ACTIVITY 4

### My Flow Activities

The idea of flow was developed by a Russian psychologist, Mihaly Csikszentmihalyi after he had spent a lot of time observing artists at work. He noticed how much the artists enjoyed their work and how, as they painted their pictures, they concentrated on arranging the colours to make a beautiful picture. The challenge of painting beautiful pictures matched the artists' ability. While they were concentrating on their painting the artists forgot about time, they forgot about eating and they forgot about bedtime, because they were so happy and engrossed in what they were doing.

The students can be encouraged to think about this word 'flow' and discuss what they think it means. They can also be encouraged to articulate and identify times when they may have experienced flow in their daily lives. What did this feel like? Were they conscious of it at the time or did they only realise that they'd experienced it after the event? What was the nature of the activity they were involved in? Was it enjoyable, physical, academic or creative?

Being 'in flow' tends to occur when the challenge of a particular activity matches our ability. When the activity is too simple we can become bored and lose interest. When it is too hard we can feel demotivated and overwhelmed and ultimately give up.

Following this initial discussion, which should hopefully ensure a shared understanding of the concept amongst the students, they can then be encouraged to complete the My Flow Activities handout. This format provides an opportunity to identify key flow activities they have alongside their enjoyable characteristics and specific challenges.

## ACTIVITY 5

### My Learning Goal Action Plan

Even 'flow' activities may include moments of anxiety or times when things get difficult and we then need to stop, reflect, evaluate our strategies and maybe begin again or take a different stance or approach. Learning to reflect upon and identify specific goals can help us to achieve. Being clear about what we want to do and setting realistic goals can help us to enjoy our learning and also enjoy working towards achieving our goals. Looking forward to achieving our goals also helps us to maintain a positive and optimistic outlook.

Students are now asked to identify one key learning goal for themselves and to identify the steps that they may need to take in order to achieve this. It is important to emphasise the fact that we all will experience setbacks and at such times we can identify alternatives in order to maintain motivation and overcome any problems. It is also important to ensure that we reward ourselves as we work towards our goal – not just when we've actually achieved it!

## Plenary

The students can finally focus upon the following questions as part of the plenary discussion:

- What have we learnt about our learning?
- What prompts us to 'love' learning new skills and using current skills?
- Why do we think learning how to learn is important?
- Do we think that personal motivators are important?
- What is flow and how do we all experience this state?
- How can we maintain a positive outlook when attempting to achieve our goals?
- Has this session been useful?
- What else would have made this session more helpful? Share ideas.

# LOVE OF LEARNING: ACTIVITY 1

## How Children Learn

John Holt said:

> The child is curious. He wants to make sense out of things, find out how things work, gain competence and control over himself and his environment, and do what he can see other people doing. He is open, perceptive and experimental. He does not shut himself off from the strange, complicated world around him, but tastes it, touches it, hefts it, bends it, breaks it. To find out how reality works, he works on it. He is bold. He is not afraid of making mistakes and he is patient. He can tolerate an extraordinary amount of uncertainty, confusion, ignorance and suspense… School is not a place that gives much time or opportunity or reward for this kind of thinking and learning.

1. Discuss this quotation together and answer the following questions:

   • Do you agree that children are naturally open, perceptive and experimental? Is this how they learn best?

   . . . . . . . . . . . . . . . . . . . . . . . . . . . . . . . . . . . . . . . . . . . . . . . . . . . . . . . . . . . . . . . . . . . . . . . . . . . . . . . . . . . . . . . . .

   . . . . . . . . . . . . . . . . . . . . . . . . . . . . . . . . . . . . . . . . . . . . . . . . . . . . . . . . . . . . . . . . . . . . . . . . . . . . . . . . . . . . . . . . .

   • What might prevent this type of learning in both a) the home, and b) the school context?

   . . . . . . . . . . . . . . . . . . . . . . . . . . . . . . . . . . . . . . . . . . . . . . . . . . . . . . . . . . . . . . . . . . . . . . . . . . . . . . . . . . . . . . . . .

   . . . . . . . . . . . . . . . . . . . . . . . . . . . . . . . . . . . . . . . . . . . . . . . . . . . . . . . . . . . . . . . . . . . . . . . . . . . . . . . . . . . . . . . . .

   • Why do you think that John Holt might feel that a school is not the best place for providing such opportunities for learning and for developing a love of learning?

   . . . . . . . . . . . . . . . . . . . . . . . . . . . . . . . . . . . . . . . . . . . . . . . . . . . . . . . . . . . . . . . . . . . . . . . . . . . . . . . . . . . . . . . . .

   . . . . . . . . . . . . . . . . . . . . . . . . . . . . . . . . . . . . . . . . . . . . . . . . . . . . . . . . . . . . . . . . . . . . . . . . . . . . . . . . . . . . . . . . .

2. Feedback to the group and discuss any similarities and differences in your views.

# John Holt's Key Principles

| **1. Children need plentiful amounts of quiet time to think** ||
|---|---|
| They need | They do not need |
| | |

| **2. Children are naturally curious and have a built-in desire to learn first-hand about the world around them** ||
|---|---|
| They need | They do not need |
| | |

| **3. Children know best how to go about learning something** ||
|---|---|
| They need | They do not need |
| | |

| **4. Children are not afraid to admit ignorance and to make mistakes** ||
|---|---|
| They need | They do not need |
| | |

| **5. Children learn best about getting along with other people through interaction with those of all ages** ||
|---|---|
| They need | They do not need |
| | |

| **6. Children take joy in the intrinsic values of whatever they are learning** ||
|---|---|
| They need | They do not need |
| | |

| **7. Children learn best about the world through first-hand experience** ||
|---|---|
| They need | They do not need |
| | |

## My Learning Motivators

Stop, think and reflect – record your Learning Motivators on the chart below.

| My Learning Motivator | When I use this | How might I use it more effectively? |
|---|---|---|
|  |  |  |

## My Flow Activities

| Flow activity What is it? | What I enjoy about it | What challenges it gives me | How I keep going/ try again if it becomes difficult |
|---|---|---|---|
|  |  |  |  |
|  |  |  |  |
|  |  |  |  |
|  |  |  |  |
|  |  |  |  |
|  |  |  |  |
|  |  |  |  |

# LOVE OF LEARNING: ACTIVITY 5

## My Learning Goal Action Plan

My learning goal is to:

This is how I plan to achieve my goal

If something doesn't work out I will have to work out a different way

These are the rewards I will give myself as I work towards my goal

| Step 1 | | Reward 1 |

| Step 2 | Alternative | Reward 2 |

| Step 3 | Alternative | Reward 3 |

| Step 4 | Alternative | Reward 4 |

# Chapter 5

# PERSPECTIVE

## BEING ABLE TO PROVIDE
## WISE COUNSEL TO OTHERS

## Introduction

In this chapter the students are introduced to the notion of perspective and why it is important to be able to think things through objectively, in order to then be able to advise both ourselves and others in our social contexts. Students are provided with an opportunity to identify their own key areas of wisdom – what is it that they know about themselves that makes them a wise person? Do they have self-knowledge? How do they behave with friends, family and those in the school context which shows that they can behave in a wise and reflective manner? This is important! We need to develop our areas of wisdom in order to then be able to provide support to others, particularly friends who may be in need or distress.

The notion of being a good friend and the qualities of good friends are also referred to within this chapter and students are further asked to engage in formulating wise counsel to others in a range of problem situations and contexts. Most importantly there is a focus upon the ways in which we listen to others. If we are truly to be able to provide wise counsel to others we need to have developed appropriate and meaningful listening skills. This is not only in the area of body language but also in the way in which we actively ask for clarification about what is being said and truly understand the speaker's feelings and situation. The final activity in this session enables students to develop a personal action plan in terms of identifying a key skill in the area of listening that they know they would like to further develop in the future.

### ACTIVITY 1

### My Areas of Wisdom

In this activity the students are asked to think about the wise thoughts or actions that they have engaged in, clarifying specific areas of wisdom in four key areas. In what ways are they wise about themselves? For example, I'm wise because I know that I've got to keep fit. I'm wise because I know my triggers to anger and things that will upset me. I'm wise because I know how to avoid and deal with certain tricky situations that induce these feelings. I may be wise with my friends because I know how to reframe their difficulties and help and support them in problem situations. I may be wise in my school context because I know how to manage teachers who are more difficult and demanding whilst also knowing how to make the most of my own talents and abilities.

I may be wise in my family context because I know how to manage some of the difficult emotions that others experience, particularly when I'm going through a state of adolescence!

This activity is hugely positive in that it confirms with students that they do have key skills in these areas. If they find this difficult it is essential that the facilitator prompts them and asks them to identify key positive thoughts, behaviours and activities that they may engage in and that they may know produce good outcomes for themselves and others.

## ACTIVITY 2

### A Friend in Need

In this activity the students are asked to consider how they currently support their friends. What is it that they do in order to show that they are good friends and to help those in need? What are the strengths that they have to be able to undertake such tasks and maintain such support systems for others? Once again this reinforces their key skills and also perhaps helps them to identify areas that they may like to improve on. For example, they may feel that they have a strength in terms of listening to others but they may also feel that they can further improve upon this particular skill, for example by not pre-judging what others are saying.

## ACTIVITY 3

### Problem Postcards

In this activity the students are once more asked to focus upon the nature of friendship and what makes a good friend. A good friend is generally one who can give wise counsel to others – this is an important skill for us. We need to be able to do this in order to maintain and further develop our friendships but we also need to recognise when certain emotions, such as jealousy, get in the way of us providing wise counsel to other people.

The students are presented with a series of scenarios which reflect problem situations. For example, Adrian says that his mum hates him because he is moody but she is always shouting at him and putting him down for not being clever. Tyrone says that he can't cope with work and school because it's too much and too difficult for him. This is making him stressed and he is therefore thinking of not turning up. The students can discuss each one of these in turn. What advice would they give to each of these individual students? Why would this be appropriate? Why would this show that they are providing wise counsel and displaying good friendship skills?

## ACTIVITY 4

### Rate Your Own Listening

In this activity the students are asked to rate their own listening skills using the following scale: 4 = always, 3 = most of the time, 2 = sometimes, 1 = never. This is an important activity in that it supports the students in the process of recognising the ways in which they do and do not listen effectively or appropriately in the social context. We need to know that we will be able to give our friends and colleagues our full attention, not fidgeting or watching others or being engaged in alternative thinking whilst someone is talking to us. We also need to be able to ask for clarification when we need to and understand how the speaker is really feeling. Students are asked to reflect upon one area that they would like to improve in particular and to then practise this over the subsequent week. They can always formulate the specific target and record this in a diary or in a notebook and then refer to it on a daily basis, identifying whether or not they've been able to improve upon this skill during each day of the week.

## Plenary

Students can finally focus upon the following questions as part of the plenary discussion:

- What have we learnt about our areas of wisdom?
- Are we wise in every area of our lives?
- Why do people need to develop these sorts of skills?
- Why is it important to support friends?
- What are our strengths in this area?
- What might prevent us from giving good advice to friends or others in our social context?
- What are the key skills of good listening?
- What do we think gets in the way of us listening appropriately to others?
- How can we further develop our skills of good listening in order to further develop and maintain our positive relationships?
- How has this session been useful?
- What else would have made this session more helpful? Share ideas.

## My Areas of Wisdom

| Self | Friends |
|---|---|
|  |  |
| **School** | **Family** |
|  |  |

## A Friend in Need

### Questions

1. How do you support your friends?
2. How do you show that you are a 'good' friend?
3. What is it that you do to help others in need?
4. What are your strengths?

### My answers

1) ..............................................................................................................

..............................................................................................................

..............................................................................................................

2) ..............................................................................................................

..............................................................................................................

..............................................................................................................

3) ..............................................................................................................

..............................................................................................................

..............................................................................................................

4) ..............................................................................................................

..............................................................................................................

..............................................................................................................

Final reflection: can you improve your skills?

..............................................................................................................

..............................................................................................................

..............................................................................................................

# PERSPECTIVE: ACTIVITY 3

## Problem Postcards

A good friend is one who can give 'wise counsel' to others. What advice would you give to these students?

| | |
|---|---|
| *Steph – 16 years*<br>I am worried because I haven't revised for my maths exam and know it is too late and I'll fail. | *Susie – 13 years*<br>My little brother says my stepdad keeps touching him when he has a bath and he doesn't like it. |
| *Alex – 12 years*<br>My mum and dad are arguing all the time and last night I heard my dad hitting my mum. | *Jordan – 12 years*<br>I am getting really fat but I just can't seem to stop eating junk food as it makes me feel better at the time. |
| *Johnnie – 13 years*<br>I am addicted to cigarettes and I just can't stop even though I want to. | *Adrian – 14 years*<br>My mum hates me because she says I am so moody but she's always shouting at me and putting me down for not being clever. |
| *Gemma – 15 years*<br>My sister is sleeping around and getting a reputation and now everyone thinks I'm just like her even though I haven't had sex with anyone. | *Tyrone – 13 years*<br>I can't cope with the work at school. It's all too much and too hard and I'm getting stressed. I'm thinking of just refusing to go. |

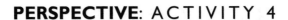

## Rate Your Own Listening

Rate your own listening skills using the following scale:

4 = always; 3 = most of the time; 2 = sometimes; 1 = never

| | | |
|---|---|---|
| 1. | I look the speaker in the eye when he or she is talking. | 1  2  3  4 |
| 2. | I can pay attention even if the subject bores me. | 1  2  3  4 |
| 3. | I wait for the speaker to finish before responding. | 1  2  3  4 |
| 4. | I keep an open mind and do not respond negatively to others' ideas or feelings. | 1  2  3  4 |
| 5. | I do more listening than talking. | 1  2  3  4 |
| 6. | I give the speaker my full attention. I do not look at my watch, fidget, do something else at the same time. | 1  2  3  4 |
| 7. | I use good non-verbal responses, for example nodding, smiling, leaning forward. | 1  2  3  4 |
| 8. | I give brief verbal responses, for example 'uh-huh' and 'mmm'. | 1  2  3  4 |
| 9. | I ask for clarification if I am unsure about what has been said. | 1  2  3  4 |
| 10. | I try to understand the speaker's feelings. | 1  2  3  4 |

Now add up your score!                                   Total = ..............

### How did you score?

| | |
|---|---|
| 10–19 | Your listening skills need to improve. Get practising – you'll soon notice an improvement. |
| 20–30 | You are doing well but there is still room for improvement. |
| Over 30 | Congratulations, you are already an excellent listener. Have a look to see if there are any areas you could improve on even more. |

### My action plan

Choose one area you would like to improve. Practise over the next week.

I would like to improve:

. . . . . . . . . . . . . . . . . . . . . . . . . . . . . . . . . . . . . . . . . . . . . . . . . . . . . . . . . . . . . . . . . . . . . . . . . . . . . . . . . .

. . . . . . . . . . . . . . . . . . . . . . . . . . . . . . . . . . . . . . . . . . . . . . . . . . . . . . . . . . . . . . . . . . . . . . . . . . . . . . . . . .

. . . . . . . . . . . . . . . . . . . . . . . . . . . . . . . . . . . . . . . . . . . . . . . . . . . . . . . . . . . . . . . . . . . . . . . . . . . . . . . . . .

# COURAGE

EMOTIONAL STRENGTHS THAT INVOLVE THE
EXERCISE OF WILL TO ACCOMPLISH GOALS IN THE
FACE OF OPPOSITION, EXTERNAL OR INTERNAL

# Chapter 6

# AUTHENTICITY

## SPEAKING THE TRUTH AND PRESENTING ONESELF IN A GENUINE WAY

## Introduction

In this chapter the students are introduced to the concept of authenticity. That is, why it is important to be real and genuine in all our social dealings and the way in which we present ourselves, and also why it is important to speak the truth in our dealings and interactions with others. The students are asked to think about how as human beings we sometimes do not show what is really there. The concept of the 'real me' is considered and the way in which we sometimes find it difficult to show who we really are to others due to a range of factors.

There is also the notion of honesty and the fact that we need to know who we are in order to present ourselves in an authentic way. This then enables us to engage in genuine responses to others and avoids the sort of dishonest presentation that ruins and damages our relationships. The students are asked to consider the ways in which they engage in honest thinking about themselves and others and how they feel about their genuine responses and behaviours over a weekly period. There is finally an opportunity to honestly consider the ways in which they would like to be in the future, identifying key aspects of their future selves in an authentic, open and honest manner so as to ensure they become the people that they really want to become.

### ACTIVITY 1

### The Real Me

In this activity the students can reflect upon the fact that we don't always show to others how we really feel. There are a variety of reasons why we may not be able to do this. Sometimes it is due to the fact that we want to avoid hurting others, and there may be some merit in such behaviours. Alternatively, we may be pretending to be something that we are not and this can create a level of dissonance that makes us feel particularly uncomfortable and ultimately is not healthy in the longer term.

Students are asked to look in the mirror and try to answer a series of questions with real honesty. These are as follows: I think I am…, I really love…, I really hate…, My best quality is…, My worst nightmare is…, I tell lies when…, I feel most positive when…, I could be happier if…, I would like to be…, I have an ambition to…

Some of these are potentially quite tricky, for example being really honest about when we tell lies. Lying is often a complex area to address. There may be times when we feel we need to lie in order to protect others but we also need to consider whether or not in the longer term protecting others by lying is potentially a useful and good strategy to be maintained.

## ACTIVITY 2
### Genuine Responses

In this activity the students are asked to focus upon the way in which we respond to others and to specific situations and prevent what we term 'dishonest presentation' in these situations. Once again there is a focus upon times when perhaps telling the truth and being authentic is more difficult than at other times. However, being authentic in the long term helps prevent the sort of dissonance that makes us feel uncomfortable and ultimately experience high levels of stress in our lives. The students are asked to consider three separate situations:

1. You have been caught cheating in an exam.
2. Your friend has told a lie about you or something that you did.
3. You took some drugs at a party and felt sick and your parents or carers have found out about it.

The students have to identify what their honest response would be in each of these situations and also what a less honest response might be and to then consider which response would be most appropriate for them. What is it that would achieve for them the best possible outcome?

## ACTIVITY 3
### My Reality Diary

In this activity the students are asked to keep a reality diary for a period of one week, recording all the times when they were a) honest to themselves, and b) honest with others and how they felt about their genuine responses and behaviours. Did these produce more positive outcomes? Did they feel more motivated as a result of being honest and responding in an authentic way? The idea here is also to reinforce the fact that feeling good often comes from behaving, thinking and responding to others in a good and positive way. There is always a pay-off in some people's view – what we give out is what we tend to receive back. This may not always be the case as we cannot always be fully aware of others' pain and anxieties at any given point in time. However, generally it is important to consider the fact that when we do act in authentic and positive ways towards others we tend to receive the same kind of positive responses back.

## ACTIVITY 4
### Future Self

In this final activity of the chapter the students are asked to consider what their best or most preferred future would be like and to visualise this and describe it in detail using the sentence starters provided on the format. The idea here is to reinforce the fact that acting and responding to others in a genuine manner and maintaining an authentic way of being in the world helps us to identify honestly what our future targets and aspirations can and should be.

## Plenary

Students can finally focus upon the following questions as part of the plenary discussion:

- What does it mean to speak the truth?

- When is it important to be truthful and honest?

- When might it be less important or is there ever a case when we should not tell the truth?

- What are the main reasons for not being authentic?

- Does being authentic, open and honest help us to maintain well-being?

- How can we further develop our skills in this area and become even more authentic in our dealings with others and in the way in which we think about ourselves?

- Has this session been useful?

- What else could have made the session more helpful? Share ideas.

# AUTHENTICITY: ACTIVITY 1

## The Real Me

Sometimes (for many reasons) we don't always show how we really feel or say what we really think to the rest of the world. Sometimes we do this to avoid hurting others and sometimes we do this because we are worried that others will not like our views or behaviours. Look in the mirror and try to answer the following questions with 'real' honesty.

I think I am

....................................................................................................................

....................................................................................................................

I really love

....................................................................................................................

....................................................................................................................

I really hate

....................................................................................................................

....................................................................................................................

My best quality is

....................................................................................................................

....................................................................................................................

My worst nightmare is

....................................................................................................................

....................................................................................................................

I tell lies when

....................................................................................................................

....................................................................................................................

I feel most positive when

....................................................................................................................

....................................................................................................................

I could be happier if

....................................................................................................................

....................................................................................................................

I would like to be

....................................................................................................................

....................................................................................................................

I have an ambition to

....................................................................................................................

....................................................................................................................

## Genuine Responses

It is important to tell the truth and to be authentic – do you agree with this statement? What would be your 'honest' response in each situation? What might be a less honest response? Why?

| Situation | Honest response | Less honest response |
|---|---|---|
| You have been caught cheating in an exam | | |
| Your friend has told a lie about you/something that you did | | |
| You took some drugs at a party and felt sick and your parents/ carers have found out | | |

# **AUTHENTICITY**: ACTIVITY 3

## My Reality Diary

|  | **Honest to self** | **Honest with others** | **How I felt** |
|---|---|---|---|
| Monday | | | |
| Tuesday | | | |
| Wednesday | | | |
| Thursday | | | |
| Friday | | | |
| Saturday | | | |
| Sunday | | | |

Keep a reality diary for a week! Record the times when you were a) honest to yourself, and b) honest with others, and how you felt about your genuine responses and behaviours.

## Future Self

What would your best or preferred future be like? Visualise this and then describe it in detail using the sentence starters below.

I will be

......................................................................................................................

......................................................................................................................

I will look like

......................................................................................................................

......................................................................................................................

I will feel like

......................................................................................................................

......................................................................................................................

I will think

......................................................................................................................

......................................................................................................................

I will act like

......................................................................................................................

......................................................................................................................

I will have

......................................................................................................................

......................................................................................................................

I will believe

......................................................................................................................

......................................................................................................................

I will be with

......................................................................................................................

......................................................................................................................

I will live

......................................................................................................................

......................................................................................................................

I will

......................................................................................................................

......................................................................................................................

# Chapter 7

# BRAVERY

## NOT SHRINKING FROM THREAT, CHALLENGE, DIFFICULTY OR PAIN

## Introduction

In this chapter the students are introduced to the concept of bravery and what it means to act in this way in the social context. The idea here is to reinforce the importance of human beings as individuals who can make a difference in their context and can frequently do so by not retreating from challenges, difficulties or situations which may cause them a certain level of pain or to experience a genuine threat. Just as acting authentically in the world helps us to maintain and further develop our positive relationships, acting in a brave manner also enables us to not act dishonestly, in terms of accepting situations that can intimidate both ourselves and others when we should clearly not do so.

The students are introduced to the notion of bravery and the variety of ways of being brave in the social world. The concept of assertiveness is also considered and their need to develop these skills in order to act in a brave way, particularly in situations of conflict and threat. The students are provided with a range of assertiveness strategies which they can then practise and further develop in the future. They are also finally asked to consider a specific challenge that they currently are experiencing which demands that they respond more bravely. This involves identifying their fears about this particular challenge and identifying specific actions that they can take in order to respond more bravely in order to achieve a better outcome in the future.

### ACTIVITY 1

### What is Bravery?

In this activity the students are required to stop, think and reflect, identifying the many different acts of bravery that people engage in on a regular basis. These can be very small acts of bravery such as standing up to read aloud in front of others when you feel that this is something that actually frightens you enormously, to helping a friend who is being bullied even though you might be frightened of being attacked yourself. There are clearly other acts of bravery in this world concerning the ways in which people, in general, stand up to injustice and intolerance – for example, racial abuse and intimidation in South Africa during the time of apartheid.

It will be useful for the facilitator or students to discuss the wide range of brave acts that they have knowledge of, including those that they themselves have performed and those that others have performed. These can then be recorded on the format provided.

## ACTIVITY 2

### Being Assertive – A Quiz

What is important when we are attempting to act in a brave manner in difficult situations is that we are socially skilled enough to present as assertive as opposed to being aggressive or passive. Students are asked to reflect on their skills by completing the quiz provided. This identifies key skills and areas for further development. For example, the following questions are posed:

- Do you often want to shout back at people?
- Do people often ignore you when you say something?
- Do you stand tall and face people openly?
- Do you find it easy to ask for help in a confident manner?

There is a simple 'yes' or 'no' response demanded and this then allows students to discuss further their responses with their facilitator. What is it that they can do to increase their assertiveness? Which specific area needs addressing now and in the future? It will also be useful to identify who can help the students and how this can be done.

## ACTIVITY 3

### Assertiveness Skills Top Tips

This information sheet and subsequent activity provides students with a series of four specific strategies for further developing assertiveness skills. These include being specific, the use of repetition, fielding responses, and engaging and finding workable compromises. The students are provided with a scenario regarding Anna, who wants to go out with her friends. She is in Year 9 at Cranford High and there is a special end-of-term party planned for the next week. Unfortunately her father refuses to let her go due to the fact that the party ends at 10.30pm and he thinks it is too late and he will be worried about her.

Students are asked to make use of the four assertiveness skills in order to engage in paired role-plays of this scenario, either with their facilitator or in pairs within the group as appropriate. They can then discuss the ways in which people achieve the best outcome. Which strategy worked best in this scenario and what are the main facts that contributed to this? It is also important to reinforce that these skills can be used by all students as appropriate in a range of different situations, when they find themselves needing to act assertively in order to get the best outcome both for themselves and others involved.

## ACTIVITY 4

### Helping Myself to Respond Bravely

In this final activity of the chapter the students are asked to identify a key challenge that they are facing, something that they may be worried about or a bit frightened of dealing with at this present time. They are then asked to engage in the stepped process:

- Step 1 requires them to identify the challenge.
- Step 2 asks them to identify fears around this.
- Step 3 asks them to provide the evidence for these fears. What is it that is contributing to this particular problem? Do they really have evidence for these fears?

- Step 4 asks what it is that they can do to change their responses. That is, what could they be doing differently?

- Step 5 asks the students to list actions that they can take in order to respond more bravely and achieve a better outcome for themselves.

This kind of stepped process to problem solving is a very useful strategy to practise and further develop, and is another tool for students to put in their toolbox of positive psychology strategies which can help them to maintain well-being both in the present and future contexts.

## Plenary

Students can finally focus upon the following questions as part of the plenary discussion:

- How can we tell when someone is being brave?

- Are there times when it's impossible to be brave?

- Are there different ways of coping with threat, challenge or difficulties?

- Does being honest and presenting oneself in a genuine and assertive way help us to maintain positive relationships?

- Does being assertive help us to deal more effectively with problem situations?

- When would it not be appropriate to be assertive?

- Has this session been useful?

- What else could have made the session more helpful? Share ideas.

# **BRAVERY**: ACTIVITY I

## What is Bravery?

There are many acts of bravery, from standing up to read aloud in front of others when you find this really frightening to helping a friend who is being bullied even though you might be frightened of being attacked yourself. Record acts of bravery in the shields on this thought-storm sheet below.

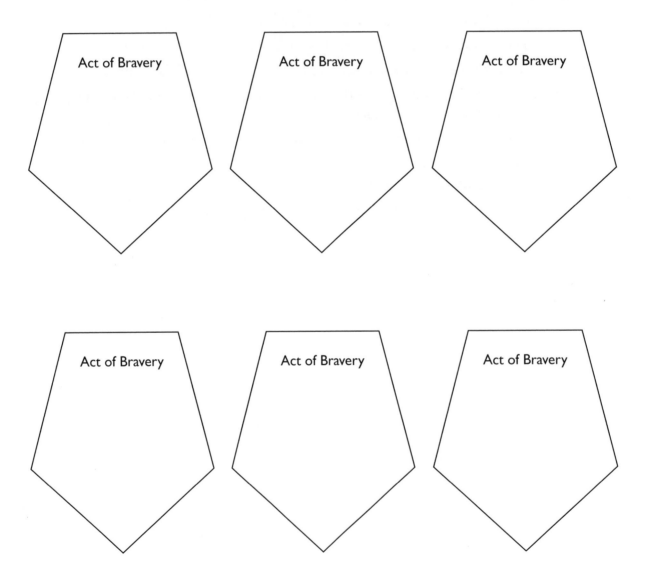

# Being Assertive – A Quiz

An important part of being socially skilled is to present as assertive and brave, neither aggressive nor passive, in more difficult situations. Reflect on your skills by completing the quiz below.

| | Yes | No |
|---|---|---|
| 1. Do you often want to shout back at people? | | |
| 2. Do you feel nervous when you have to ask for something? | | |
| 3. Do you blame yourself when plans do not work out well? | | |
| 4. If someone pushes you out in a queue do you speak up? | | |
| 5. Do people often ignore you when you say something? | | |
| 6. When you do not understand what the teachers say do you ask for an explanation? | | |
| 7. Do you stand tall and face people openly? | | |
| 8. Do you buy clothes you do not want because a salesperson puts you under pressure? | | |
| 9. Do you find it easy to ask for help in a confident manner? | | |
| 10. Do you look people in the face when you talk to them? | | |

Stop, think and reflect. Discuss your responses with your facilitator. What can you do to increase your assertiveness? Who can help you? How?

# BRAVERY: ACTIVITY 3

## Assertiveness Skills Top Tips

1. Be specific

   Decide what it is you want to express and say so specifically and directly. Be clear. Be brief.

2. Repetition

   This skill helps you to stay with your statement or request by using calm repetition, over and over again.

3. Fielding the response

   Indicate that you have heard what the other person says so that you do not get 'hooked' by what they say. This skill helps you to acknowledge what the other person has said and still continue confidently with your statement.

4. Workable compromise

   When your needs are in conflict with the needs and wishes of someone else, it is important to find a true compromise which considers you both.

## Scenario

> Anna wants to go out with her friends. She is in Year 9 at Cranford High and there is a special end-of-term party next week. Her dad says she cannot go as the party ends at 10.30pm and this is too late. He says he will be worried about her.

## Activity

Use the four assertiveness skills above in paired role-plays of this scenario with your facilitator or someone else in your group. Perform these role-plays in turn and then discuss the ways in which people achieved the best outcome. What are the main factors that contributed to this?

## BRAVERY: ACTIVITY 4

# Helping Myself to Respond Bravely

Identify a key challenge that you are facing – something that you may be worried about or a bit frightened of dealing with. Work through the stepped process below.

Step 1 – Your challenge

..................................................................................................................

..................................................................................................................

Step 2 – Fears about this

..................................................................................................................

..................................................................................................................

Step 3 – What is the evidence for these fears?

..................................................................................................................

..................................................................................................................

Step 4 – What can you do to change your responses/what can you do differently?

..................................................................................................................

..................................................................................................................

Step 5 – List the actions you can take in order to response more bravely and achieve a better outcome:

Action 1

..................................................................................................................

Action 2

..................................................................................................................

Action 3

..................................................................................................................

Action 4

..................................................................................................................

COPYRIGHT © RUTH MACCONVILLE AND TINA RAE 2012

# Chapter 8

# PERSISTENCE

## FINISHING WHAT ONE STARTS

## Introduction

In this chapter the students are introduced to the concept of persistence and the need and importance we place on actually finishing tasks that we begin and persevering, even when things get difficult and it seems virtually impossible to reach our goals or achieve our aspirations. We need to be able to reflect carefully and sensitively upon the ways in which we've responded in the past. For example, there may be things that we didn't complete in our lives in the way that we would have liked to. We need to understand and identify why this was the case, in order to then move forward in the future, and identify what we could do differently in the same situation another time.

Sometimes it is far too easy to set unrealistic goals and this then causes us to become quickly demotivated and lacking in persistence. It is vital that as human beings we identify goals that can be achieved and also the process by which they can be achieved. Consequently this chapter aims to support students in this process, providing them with a stepped problem-solving format which enables them to specifically identify resources and smaller targets in order to achieve the bigger goals that they may have in life. In order to do this it is essential that they can remain motivated and persistent, and part of this process involves focusing on hope and maintaining hopeful thoughts in our minds as we progress in our life's journey.

### ACTIVITY 1

### What Didn't I Finish?

In this activity the students are asked to consider a series of activities or tasks that they didn't complete previously. They are asked to clarify what it was that hindered them in this process and also to consider what might have helped them. What was it that they or others could have done in order to make this task more achievable so that they could then complete it?

They are finally asked to consider what they could do differently in a similar situation. This is particularly important. When things go wrong it is always important to identify why exactly that happened but also to consider alternative future options. What could I do differently in the future in order to not get myself in this situation again? What could I do differently in the future in order to achieve a better outcome? What could I do differently in the future in order to complete this task rather than give up halfway through? Answers to these questions will clearly involve identifying more realistic goals and steps by which to achieve those goals which can be conducted in a logical and achievable manner.

## ACTIVITY 2

### Setting 'Real' Goals – Climb the Mountain

In this activity the students are encouraged to identify their own goals. These are written or drawn on a piece of paper and then cut out and arranged on the format provided. This presents them with a picture of a mountain. They are asked to place the ones that seem easiest to achieve at the bottom of the mountain, the most difficult at the top and the slightly easier ones in the middle. They are then asked to start with the first and easiest task and when they've achieved this they can then climb a little further up the mountain and try the next one. The idea here is to reinforce the fact that we can have very big goals in our lives but we need to take small steps in order to achieve them and this is a process that will take time and will mean building upon our skills as we go along.

## ACTIVITY 3

### Be a Finisher – Seven-step Problem Solver

Once again this activity reinforces the need to clarify and identify small achievable steps on the way to reaching our goals. If we do this we can maintain our level of motivation and be persistent and we can also finish what we have begun in terms of identifying our goals and starting the process of achieving them. The students are asked to use the format in order to solve a problem that they have currently that involves finishing something that they started:

- Step 1 involves describing the problem.
- Step 2 involves visualising life without the problem. What this would look like. This is a very powerful tool. When we can visualise life without the problem we can tackle step 3.
- Step 3 involves identifying key things that the students can do in order to reach the state of life without the problem.
- Step 4 then asks them to identify specific resources that will help them in this process.
- Step 5 asks them to identify potential problems and plan for these, that is, 'What would happen if…?'
- Step 6 then asks them to once again visualise success. How will they know when the problem is solved?
- Step 7 encourages students to identify how confident they currently feel that this problem could be solved if they take the actions that they've described to date.

## ACTIVITY 4

### Focus on Hope – It Helps to Keep You Persistent

This activity again reinforces the need to remain hopeful, as this state of being helps us to maintain a level of persistence that allows us to reach our goals and achieve what we want to achieve. Students are asked to define hope and then to complete a range of sentence starters which will focus upon future hopes, both for themselves and others. These can then be discussed with the facilitator and/or other people in the group in order to identify any similarities and differences but also to focus upon what is hopeful about each of these statements and how some of these hopes might be realised in the future.

# Plenary

Students can finally focus upon the following questions as part of the plenary discussion:

- What does being persistent mean?
- What makes it difficult for us to finish things that we've begun?
- What kinds of challenges do we experience?
- What helps us to achieve our goals?
- Why is it useful to have realistic goals and break these down into smaller steps?
- What is the best way of coping when things go wrong and we seem to have missed a step and fallen backwards?
- How can we get back onto the next step in order to achieve our goals?
- Why is being hopeful so important in life?
- Has this session been useful?
- What else could have made the session more helpful? Share ideas.

# PERSISTENCE: ACTIVITY 1

## What Didn't I Finish?

| Task/activity | What hindered? | What might have helped? | What could I do differently next time? |
|---|---|---|---|
|  |  |  |  |
|  |  |  |  |
|  |  |  |  |
|  |  |  |  |

## Setting 'Real' Goals – Climb the Mountain

Write or draw all your goals on a piece of paper. Cut them out and then arrange them on the mountain below. Place the ones that seem easiest to achieve at the bottom, the most difficult at the top and the slightly easier ones in the middle. Next, start with the first and easiest task. When you've achieved it, climb a little further up the mountain and try the next one. Remember, take small steps to reach the top!

# Be a Finisher – Seven Step Problem Solver

Use the format to begin to solve a problem that you have that involves finishing something that you have started.

Step 1 – Describe the problem

................................................................................................................

................................................................................................................

Step 2 – Visualise life without the problem. What would it look like? How would you think, feel and act and how would others respond?

................................................................................................................

................................................................................................................

Step 3 – Take action! Identify three key things you can do in order to reach the state of life without the problem.

1) ..............................................................................................................

2) ..............................................................................................................

3) ..............................................................................................................

Step 4 – Identify resources. Who else could help you? How?

................................................................................................................

................................................................................................................

Step 5 – Identify potential problems and plan. What would happen if…?

................................................................................................................

................................................................................................................

Step 6 – Visualise success. How will you know when your problem is solved? How will others know when your problem is solved?

................................................................................................................

................................................................................................................

Step 7 – Be confident. How confident are you now that this problem can be solved if you take action?

................................................................................................................

................................................................................................................

## Focus on Hope – It Helps to Keep You Persistent

My definition of hope is

..........................................................................................................

..........................................................................................................

I hope I will always feel

..........................................................................................................

..........................................................................................................

In the future I hope I will have a job as

..........................................................................................................

..........................................................................................................

In the future, I hope that my friends

..........................................................................................................

..........................................................................................................

I hope that everyone in my family

..........................................................................................................

..........................................................................................................

I hope I can be better at

..........................................................................................................

..........................................................................................................

I hope I won't become

..........................................................................................................

..........................................................................................................

I hope this world will be

..........................................................................................................

..........................................................................................................

I hope I will be

..........................................................................................................

..........................................................................................................

# Chapter 9

# ZEST

## APPROACHING LIFE WITH EXCITEMENT AND ENERGY

## Introduction

In this chapter the students are asked to consider the concept of zest. What is it that enables us to approach life with both excitement and energy? Why is this such an important way of being? Clearly there are implications for our overall well-being here in that being zestful and positive and excited about life in general certainly helps us to maintain both emotional and mental well-being. It is vital that students understand this fact and can feel excited about themselves, their lives and what is going on in the world around and want to engage in the positive aspects of being.

Students are initially asked to identify the kinds of things that excite them in their life. What is it that makes them want to become engaged and act in an authentic and highly motivated way? Identifying key energisers and motivators is important in this process as we need to know what actually induces these kinds of feelings and behaviours since clearly this is something that we would all want more of in our lives. It is therefore important that we know what our triggers and zest are so that we can then surround ourselves with such triggers and avoid those that produce the opposite kinds of feelings and behaviours. These are the kinds of bad habits that we need to use our energy on in order to eradicate them from our lives.

Consequently, the students are asked to engage in identifying bad habits that they want to dump and to record small steps in the process of achieving such a goal. There is finally opportunity to identify a specific challenge and to maintain and further develop the zest and motivation to achieve this challenge without giving up.

### ACTIVITY I

### What Excites Me?

In this activity the students are asked to consult with their facilitator and/or others in the group in order to identify the key things that excite them and motivate them in their lives. They can also then consider how they can maintain this kind of zest for life even when the things that help them maintain this state of being don't always happen. There is a real need to emphasise the fact that when we surround ourselves with positive situations, contexts and people we tend to be able to maintain this level of zest and motivation on a much more persistent basis.

## ACTIVITY 2

### My Key Energisers and Motivators

In this activity the students are asked to identify people, situations and particular circumstances, hobbies, interests or passions that particularly energise and motivate them. This is really important as the key energisers and motivators that they have are the things that will help them to maintain emotional and mental well-being. These are things that keep us healthy and happy.

The students are asked to identify key energisers and motivators and also to clarify whether these are potentially healthy or unhealthy. For example, some students may say that they are motivated by taking drugs or smoking and that this is something that helps to make them feel energised. It's particularly important not to condemn such behaviour in the sense that the student has actually identified this for themselves; however, it is important to help them to appreciate whether or not this is a healthy or unhealthy option. In the longer term it is important that these key energisers do have healthy benefits for us, both physically and emotionally, and that the outcome is therefore the best possible outcome for ourselves. So, for example, when considering the issue of smoking or drugs we know that this is unhealthy and we also know that the best possible outcome isn't always achieved. We may feel less stressed initially and we may feel that we are calmer in a certain situation but in the longer term there are potential fatal health effects.

## ACTIVITY 3

### Use Your Energy and Bin It!

In this activity the students are asked to identify all the kinds of bad habits that they have and put these in order, with the easiest to stop or prevent at the bottom and the hardest at the top. This reinforces the smoking example which might be provided to the students in the previous activity. They are asked to identify one habit that they want to get rid of and to then record small steps to success.

Once again this notion of breaking down tasks into smaller, more achievable steps is emphasised. In this way we can really see progress and we can also begin to achieve these bigger goals and dump those bigger bad habits that we find so problematic. There is also an opportunity to consider how students can remain calm in the process and what kind of coping self-talk they may have. They could always identify a script with their facilitator and this can be recorded on the format provided. It is also important to identify other resources. Who else can help and support them, and how?

## ACTIVITY 4

### Keep the Excitement and Take Up the Challenge

Once again a stepped process is presented in order to help students take up a main challenge in their lives. They can identify that challenge, which may or may not be getting rid of a bad habit as in the previous activity. In this activity it could possibly be a future challenge or objective that is something really positive that they want to achieve. They are then asked to identify small steps to success and also engage in coping self-talk, visualisation and an experiment in terms of picking a time to face up to this challenge and trying out the steps that they've identified in this process. Stage 5 involves giving themselves a reward, and once again this is important. We need to continually reward ourselves for the achievements that we make, no matter how small, and these rewards should be provided by ourselves and others at every step of the journey on the challenge.

## Plenary

Students can finally focus upon the following questions as part of the plenary discussion:

- What have we learnt about the concept of zest?
- How easy is it to approach life with excitement and energy at all times?
- What stops us from doing this in our lives?
- What's the best way of maintaining a good level of zest and motivation?
- Is it important to avoid things that drain our energy?
- Is it vital that we identify and surround ourselves with people who give us energy and make us feel zestful?
- How easy is it to bin bad habits, and does the stepped process help?
- What kinds of challenges have we identified for ourselves and how confident do we feel that we can take these up and go with them?
- Has this session been useful?
- What else could have made the session more helpful? Share ideas.

# ZEST: ACTIVITY 1

## What Excites Me?

What excites me?

Discuss with your facilitator! Consider how you maintain a 'zest' for life even when the things that excite you occur less frequently.

# ZEST: ACTIVITY 2

## My Key Energisers and Motivators

These can be people, situations, particular circumstances, hobbies, interests, passions, etc. Consider your key energisers and motivators and identify if these are healthy or unhealthy. Then think about which of these really achieves the best possible outcome.

| Key energiser/motivator | Healthy/unhealthy | Does it achieve the 'best' possible outcome? |
|---|---|---|
| | | |
| | | |
| | | |
| | | |
| | | |
| | | |

## Use Your Energy and Bin It!

Bin that bad habit! Use the small steps.

On the back of this page write down all your 'bad' habits and put them in order – easiest to stop at the bottom and hardest at the top.

Pick one habit to dump

. . . . . . . . . . . . . . . . . . . . . . . . . . . . . . . . . . . . . . . . . . . . . . . . . . . . . . . . . . . . . . . . . . . . . . . . . . . . . . . . . . . . . . . . . . . . . . . . .

Record your small steps to success

1) . . . . . . . . . . . . . . . . . . . . . . . . . . . . . . . . . . . . . . . . . . . . . . . . . . . . . . . . . . . . . . . . . . . . . . . . . . . . . . . . . . . . .

. . . . . . . . . . . . . . . . . . . . . . . . . . . . . . . . . . . . . . . . . . . . . . . . . . . . . . . . . . . . . . . . . . . . . . . . . . . . . . . . . . . . . . . .

2) . . . . . . . . . . . . . . . . . . . . . . . . . . . . . . . . . . . . . . . . . . . . . . . . . . . . . . . . . . . . . . . . . . . . . . . . . . . . . . . . . . . . .

. . . . . . . . . . . . . . . . . . . . . . . . . . . . . . . . . . . . . . . . . . . . . . . . . . . . . . . . . . . . . . . . . . . . . . . . . . . . . . . . . . . . . . . .

3) . . . . . . . . . . . . . . . . . . . . . . . . . . . . . . . . . . . . . . . . . . . . . . . . . . . . . . . . . . . . . . . . . . . . . . . . . . . . . . . . . . . . .

. . . . . . . . . . . . . . . . . . . . . . . . . . . . . . . . . . . . . . . . . . . . . . . . . . . . . . . . . . . . . . . . . . . . . . . . . . . . . . . . . . . . . . . .

4) . . . . . . . . . . . . . . . . . . . . . . . . . . . . . . . . . . . . . . . . . . . . . . . . . . . . . . . . . . . . . . . . . . . . . . . . . . . . . . . . . . . . .

. . . . . . . . . . . . . . . . . . . . . . . . . . . . . . . . . . . . . . . . . . . . . . . . . . . . . . . . . . . . . . . . . . . . . . . . . . . . . . . . . . . . . . . .

How will you keep calm? What is your coping self-talk?

. . . . . . . . . . . . . . . . . . . . . . . . . . . . . . . . . . . . . . . . . . . . . . . . . . . . . . . . . . . . . . . . . . . . . . . . . . . . . . . . . . . . . . . .

. . . . . . . . . . . . . . . . . . . . . . . . . . . . . . . . . . . . . . . . . . . . . . . . . . . . . . . . . . . . . . . . . . . . . . . . . . . . . . . . . . . . . . . .

. . . . . . . . . . . . . . . . . . . . . . . . . . . . . . . . . . . . . . . . . . . . . . . . . . . . . . . . . . . . . . . . . . . . . . . . . . . . . . . . . . . . . . . .

. . . . . . . . . . . . . . . . . . . . . . . . . . . . . . . . . . . . . . . . . . . . . . . . . . . . . . . . . . . . . . . . . . . . . . . . . . . . . . . . . . . . . . . .

Who else can help or support you and how?

. . . . . . . . . . . . . . . . . . . . . . . . . . . . . . . . . . . . . . . . . . . . . . . . . . . . . . . . . . . . . . . . . . . . . . . . . . . . . . . . . . . . . . . .

. . . . . . . . . . . . . . . . . . . . . . . . . . . . . . . . . . . . . . . . . . . . . . . . . . . . . . . . . . . . . . . . . . . . . . . . . . . . . . . . . . . . . . . .

. . . . . . . . . . . . . . . . . . . . . . . . . . . . . . . . . . . . . . . . . . . . . . . . . . . . . . . . . . . . . . . . . . . . . . . . . . . . . . . . . . . . . . . .

. . . . . . . . . . . . . . . . . . . . . . . . . . . . . . . . . . . . . . . . . . . . . . . . . . . . . . . . . . . . . . . . . . . . . . . . . . . . . . . . . . . . . . . .

Have a go! Reward yourself and don't give up! Go for it!

# Keep the Excitement and Take Up the Challenge!

My main challenge

..............................................................................................

..............................................................................................

Stage 1 – My steps to succeed

1) ...........................................................................................

..............................................................................................

2) ...........................................................................................

..............................................................................................

3) ...........................................................................................

..............................................................................................

4) ...........................................................................................

..............................................................................................

Stage 2 – My coping self-talk

..............................................................................................

..............................................................................................

Stage 3 – Visualise yourself being successful
*Repeat your coping self-talk while you imagine reaching your first step. Keep practising this.*

Stage 4 – Experiment!
*Pick a time to face your fear or challenge. Try it out. Take your first step and use your self-talk.*

Stage 5 – Reward!
*Treat yourself for being successful.*

Don't give up! Keep going! Break the steps down into smaller ones if you don't succeed.

# Virtue Three

## HUMANITY

### INTERPERSONAL STRENGTHS THAT INVOLVE 'TENDING AND BEFRIENDING' OTHERS

# Chapter 10

# KINDNESS

## DOING FAVOURS AND GOOD DEEDS TO OTHERS

## Introduction

In this chapter the students are introduced to the concept of kindness and the importance of acting in a kind way to others and also to oneself. There is an opportunity to distinguish between the empathy involved in being kind as opposed to sympathy for others who are in distress or difficulty. There is a distinct difference here and students need to be made aware of the fact that acting in a kind, authentic way to others and showing them empathy is a healthy way of responding in relationships and maintaining and further developing positive relationships in our lives. Understanding how other people feel and knowing how we might feel towards them in each of these situations, or how we might feel if we were in their shoes, is vital. We need to be able to see a situation from someone else's viewpoint in order to then help them to cope with the situation more effectively and also to be able to identify the kind of support and kindness that we can show to them in order to help them and make things better.

It is also important that we become increasingly aware of the need to be kind to ourselves. Very often we can reduce stress by engaging in a range of activities which are self-nurturing – this is not selfish. These are patterns of behaviour that enable us to maintain our well-being and therefore have the strength and resilience in order to support and be kind to others. It is also vital that we understand the need to show such kindness on a regular or almost daily basis. Engaging in kind activities and seeing the positive outcomes that ensue helps to further maintain and bolster our own self-esteem and also provides us with a feel-good factor that helps us to maintain a positive outlook and stance in our lives.

## ACTIVITY 1

### Defining Kindness

In this activity the students can be asked 'What is kindness?' and to then record their ideas on the format provided. The important aspect of this activity is to identify the range of different kind acts that we can make or that can be made towards us. These can range from very small things such as opening a door for someone who is disabled, telling someone that we love them or appreciate what they've done, or actually engaging in charitable acts on a longer-term or more consistent basis. It's important that students realise that all of these acts of kindness do count and make a difference both to themselves and others in their lives.

**ACTIVITY 2**

### Empathy or Sympathy?

This is an important distinction for students to be able to understand. Empathy is not sympathy – it is a conscious choice to step out of our own world and into those of other people. In this way we have to leave behind our own beliefs, values and attitudes in order to accept the others in a non-judgemental way. This is the kind of skill we need to develop in order to maintain positive relationships and also help ourselves and others through the change process.

The students are asked to look at a series of empathy cards. These detail ten different situations in which young people are experiencing significant difficulties. For example, George has just left his mum in hospital; she is suffering from manic depression and now has to be kept in hospital for eight weeks. In the meantime George has to look after his little brother and sister and to try to get to school as well. The students are asked to consider a series of questions related to each of the empathy cards. It may be useful to select just one or two of the empathy cards for consideration if time is limited.

**ACTIVITY 3**

### Be Kind to Yourself – A List of Kind Acts

We can reduce stress by engaging in hobbies, spending time with friends, listening to music, etc. It is important that the students know how to look after themselves – in essence, by being kind to themselves and engaging in the sorts of behaviours that make them feel good. This is not a selfish act, but a protective means of keeping strong and positive, and also enables us to subsequently be strong and positive for others when they feel down.

The students are asked to record the ways in which they know that they are kind to themselves. What is it that they do to protect and maintain their well-being? This could include going to the gym, listening to music, talking with friends, swimming, dancing, and eating favourite foods.

**ACTIVITY 4**

### A Daily Act of Kindness

In this activity the students are asked to identify a kind act that they completed for each day of the week. What was this act? What was the outcome and what were their thoughts and feelings about it? The idea here is to reinforce the fact that doing good, being kind in the world, helps us not only to become better, more positive and motivated people but also has a significant impact on others. Once again, what we give out in terms of good, positive emotions, feelings and behaviours tends to be returned to us by those who have been on the receiving end of these acts of kindness.

## Plenary

Students can finally focus upon the following questions as part of the plenary discussion:

- What is our definition of kindness?
- Why is it important to be kind?

- Can kindness ever be equated with weakness?
- What is the difference between empathy and sympathy?
- What difference does being empathic make to our relationships?
- Why is it important to be kind to ourselves?
- What is the difference between nurturing ourselves in a positive way and nurturing ourselves in a negative way?
- What sorts of self-nurture are best for each of us?
- Has this session been useful?
- What else could have made the session more helpful? Share ideas.

## Defining Kindness

What is kindness? Record your ideas!

**Kindness is...**

## Empathy or Sympathy?

Empathy is not sympathy. It is a conscious choice to step out of your own 'world' and into that of someone else. You leave behind your beliefs, values and attitudes in order to accept theirs in a non-judgemental way.

We need to develop this skill in order to develop positive relationships and to help ourselves and others through the change process.

Look carefully at each of the empathy cards. Work on your own to answer the following questions:

1. How does this person feel?

2. How do you think they make others who care about them feel?

3. How would you feel if you were in their shoes?

4. What would you be thinking?

5. How would you behave?

6. What support or help might you want?

7. What support or help wouldn't you want?

8. What would you want to happen?

9. How would you begin to make this happen?

10. How would other people know that you were feeling differently or that a change had been made?

Compare your ideas with a partner or discuss with your facilitator. Where are the similarities and differences? How do you feel about each other's' ideas and responses?

# KINDNESS: ACTIVITY 2

## Empathy Cards

| | |
|---|---|
| *Empathy Card 1*<br>George has just left his mum in hospital. She is suffering with manic depression and has to be kept in hospital for eight weeks. He has to look after his little brother and sister and try to get to school as well. | *Empathy Card 2*<br>Geraldine started smoking three years ago when she was 13. She can't seem to break the habit and it is expensive and has given her a bad cough. Her best friend tells her she smells like an ashtray and she knows it's true. |
| *Empathy Card 3*<br>Michael is behind with all his course work. He is considering just dropping out of school altogether because the pressure is just too much for him. | *Empathy Card 4*<br>Jean has put on three stone in weight since her gran died of cancer. She can't seem to stop eating. People at school have started bullying her because of this. |
| *Empathy Card 5*<br>Shahin and his family managed to get out of Afghanistan and come to this country as political refugees. He saw most of his family being murdered and now he's here he is continually abused by peers in school who say he is a terrorist. | *Empathy Card 6*<br>Mark has known that he is gay since he was 12. Now he wants to be open about it but there are lots of homophobic students in his year group and he is scared. |
| *Empathy Card 7*<br>Emma's mum has got a new boyfriend who keeps trying to tell her what to do. He is aggressive and shouts a lot. Emma consequently doesn't feel like going home from school. | *Empathy Card 8*<br>Joleen finds all her work really hard and has started to act up in class to cover up the fact that she can't do the work. She has just been given a five day fixed-term exclusion for not completing her work. |
| *Empathy Card 9*<br>Ben's gran is dying from a terminal illness. She has looked after him since he was a baby. He doesn't want to go to school as he wants to spend what time she has left being with her and looking after her, but school staff say he cannot do this and want him in school. | *Empathy Card 10*<br>Max's six-year-old little brother has a cleft palate and has already had eight operations to date. He has told Max that other children in his class won't play with him and call him the Ugly Alien – amongst other things. |

# Be Kind to Yourself – A List of Kind Acts

We can reduce stress by enjoying hobbies, spending time with friends and listening to music. It is important that we know how to look after ourselves – in essence, by being 'kind' to ourselves. This keeps us strong and positive and enables us to also be strong and positive for others when they feel down.

Record the ways in which you are kind to yourself! What do you do to protect and maintain your well-being?

| Kind act | How this helps me |
|---|---|
|  |  |
|  |  |
|  |  |
|  |  |
|  |  |
|  |  |
|  |  |

## A Daily Act of Kindness

| | **Act of kindness – what was it?** | **Outcome – what happened?** | **Review – my thoughts and feelings** |
|---|---|---|---|
| Monday | | | |
| Tuesday | | | |
| Wednesday | | | |
| Thursday | | | |
| Friday | | | |
| Saturday | | | |
| Sunday | | | |

# Chapter 11

# LOVE

## VALUING CLOSE RELATIONS WITH OTHERS

## Introduction

In this chapter students are introduced to the concept of love and the importance of valuing close relationships with others. The idea here is to reinforce the importance of authentic, loving relationships with people in our social contexts and the ways in which we can show love to others and ensure that we maintain and further develop our positive relationships in our lives. The students are asked to define love in the first instance, identifying all the different kinds of love that we may experience. This can be emotional, physical love that comes from sincere friendship and acts of love that we perform in order to show others that we care about them.

The concept and importance of loving oneself is also emphasised. In order to maintain our emotional and mental well-being and to further promote our sense of self-esteem and importance in the world, it is important that we have a level of self-regard that is appropriate to this task.

Sometimes we can engage in thinking or behaviours that are slightly irrational and that produce negative feelings and emotions in others. It is important that we are aware of these and can identify when we are behaving in such an inauthentic and negative way. It is also important that we know and can control our emotions and that we can be self-disciplined in the way that we respond to others so as to ensure both our own and their well-being. It is vital that as human beings we can identify a circle of loved ones, people who can support us and whom we support and love in return. This is important because it is this kind of network that helps us to maintain our well-being. It is also vital that we engage in daily acts of love and loving imagination towards others. This is what helps to keep us positive and maintain our well-being overall.

### ACTIVITY 1

### Love Is

In this thought-storm activity the students are asked to identify all the different forms of love that they may experience and show in their lives. How would they define this concept or way of being? How would they define these behaviours? What is important is to make the distinction between loving others for the right reasons and not for the wrong reasons. We don't show love for others so that we can gain control over them, we show love for them so that we also seek and receive love in return.

## ACTIVITY 2

### Love Thyself!

In this activity the students are asked to consider a series of statements in turn and to discuss these with their facilitator or to discuss them with others in the group.

The students are asked to identify how the person who is making each statement feels, and then to consider how true this statement would be, and finally to identify how true this statement would be for them. For example, 'People must love me or I will be devastated.' How important is this for someone else? Why would they feel this way and also how important is it for me? Do I really feel that people must always love me and that all the people in my life must love me or else I will be devastated? Are there times in which it's not so important that I have these feelings from others directed towards me?

Finally the students are asked to reflect upon overall how positive they feel about themselves. Do they feel in control of themselves and do they love themselves enough? This is vital. It is very difficult to show love and to perform acts of loving imagination towards others when we do not love ourselves.

## ACTIVITY 3

### My Circle of Loved Ones

In this activity the students are asked to identify people who are within their circle of loved ones. These could include people such as parents or carers, true close friends, people that love them because they help and support them in the school or learning context or in other contexts. They are asked to clarify why these people have been placed in this circle and also to think about how they show their love towards these people. If these people love them then it is clearly the case that very often they will be showing acts of kindness and love too. They can identify also how these people show love to them. This is a hugely positive activity to engage in. It reinforces one's self-worth and self-esteem.

## ACTIVITY 4

### Daily Acts of Love and Loving Imagination

In order to remain positive about ourselves and others it is important that we engage in daily acts of love and loving imagination and kindness towards others. This reinforces previous activities in this area of positive psychology, which are based upon the premise that what we give to others is generally what we tend to receive back, unless of course the others are hugely damaged and finding things difficult in their lives themselves.

The students are asked to identify a series of loving acts that they can perform on a daily basis for each day of the week. They are asked to identify who would benefit from these acts and then to specify exactly when they will perform this act. For example, if they know it would be beneficial to get up early and make the breakfast for their mum and that this would be something that she'd really appreciate and would make her feel loved, they can then set a time and date on which to act upon this and perform this act of loving imagination.

## Plenary

Students can finally focus upon the following questions as part of the plenary discussion:

- How would we define love?
- Why is it important to love others?
- Why is it important to be loved?
- Do we feel that we love ourselves enough?
- Are there areas in our lives in which we need to love ourselves more and nurture ourselves in a better way?
- Who is in our circle of loved ones?
- Why is it important to perform daily acts of love and loving imagination?
- What would happen if people in the world did not do this?
- Has this session been useful?
- What else could have made the session more helpful? Share ideas.

## Love Is

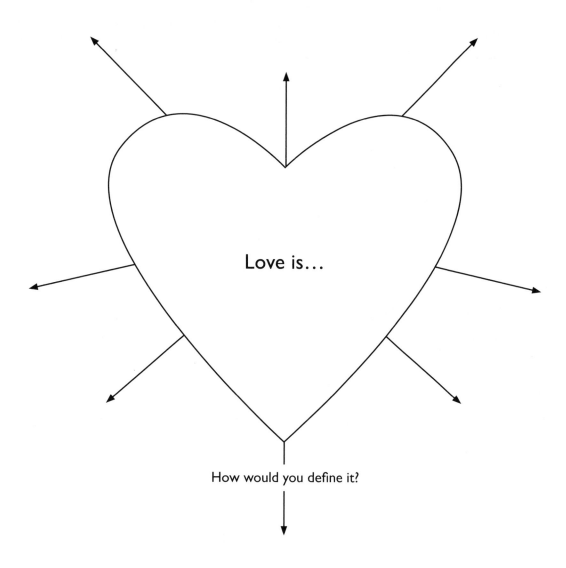

Love is…

How would you define it?

# Love Thyself!

Discuss each statement in turn with your facilitator/in your group and complete columns 1 and 2. Then complete column 3.

|  | (1)<br>How does this person feel? | (2)<br>How true is this statement? | (3)<br>How true is this of/for me? |
|---|---|---|---|
| People must love me or I will be devastated. |  |  |  |
| Making mistakes is not an option. |  |  |  |
| My emotions cannot be controlled, it's just impossible. |  |  |  |
| It is too difficult to be self-disciplined all the time. |  |  |  |
| I can't stand the way others act in my class. |  |  |  |
| Every problem has a perfect solution that can be found. |  |  |  |
| I can't change what I think, feel and do. |  |  |  |
| If others pay attention to me I must have done something bad. |  |  |  |
| I must never show any sign of weakness. |  |  |  |
| Sane people don't get upset. |  |  |  |
| You can't tell me anything about myself that I don't know already. |  |  |  |
| I must be happy all the time. |  |  |  |
| It is the job of other people to solve my problems. |  |  |  |

Stop, think and reflect. Overall, how positive do you feel about yourself? Do you feel in control of yourself and do you 'love' yourself enough?

## My Circle of Loved Ones

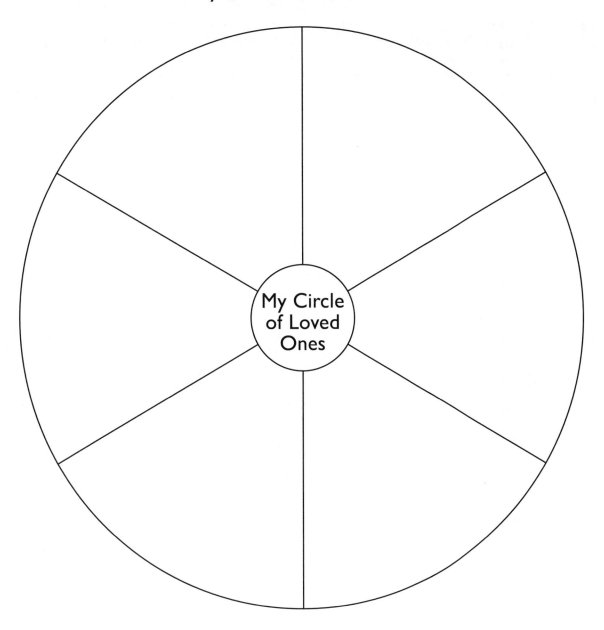

- Who is in your circle and why?

- How do you show your love to them?

- How do they show their love to you?

# Daily Acts of Love and Loving Imagination

| | My act of loving imagination | Who benefits? Name them | When shall I do this? Set a date! |
|---|---|---|---|
| Monday | | | |
| Tuesday | | | |
| Wednesday | | | |
| Thursday | | | |
| Friday | | | |
| Saturday | | | |
| Sunday | | | |

# Chapter 12

# SOCIAL INTELLIGENCE

## BEING AWARE OF THE MOTIVES AND FEELINGS OF SELF AND OTHERS

## Introduction

In this chapter the students are introduced to the concept of social intelligence and the importance of developing our skills in this area in order to maintain and further foster positive relationships and overall well-being. It is vital that we can be aware of the motives and feelings of both ourselves and others in the social context. In this way we can act more intelligently and more authentically in our dealings with other people.

Students are asked to consider a range of different emotions and to identify how comfortable each of these feelings would be for themselves and others. It is important that we know how we feel, how we are responding and the ways in which we can cope more effectively with feelings that are uncomfortable. This relates also to the way in which we show friendship and love towards other people. In order to do this we need to have a range of good social skills and students are asked to reflect upon their skills in this area alongside identifying why people perform certain acts in their lives, whether these are loving acts or unloving acts.

It is also vital that we can read others, in the sense of not just empathising with them but also recognising their levels of social intelligence and their motivations for doing things that they are engaged in. It is vital that we look at people who are socially skilled and try to learn from their behaviours and responses. Being socially skilled enables us to perform successfully within the world and also helps us to maintain and further foster and develop our overall well-being.

### ACTIVITY I

### How Do They Feel...?

In this activity the students are presented with a series of word cards which list a range of emotions as follows:

- Thoughtful
- Disgusted
- Determined
- Loving
- Angry

- Shy
- Hopeful
- Caring
- Tearful.

The students are asked to list the situations in order of comfort and write their ranking in the box beside each of the words. They are asked to start with the most comfortable and end with the least comfortable. They can then discuss the skills and strategies that they think a person should use when they are feeling withdrawn and lonely. What is it that they would suggest? How could a person deal with and cope more effectively with uncomfortable feelings? This is vital – it is an essential life skill. We need to know how to cope when we are experiencing negative feelings and we need to know that we can reflect upon these and try to find a way forward.

## ACTIVITY 2

### My Friendship Skills

In this activity the students are introduced to a range of qualities that depict or are representative of a person who is good at friendship. They are required to look at the friendship qualities recorded on the activity sheet and rate themselves against each one (1 being not very often, 3 being quite often and 5 being all the time).

The idea here is for students to then identify three areas that they would like to improve upon and develop further. What is it that they need to do and who can help them? This can be discussed with the facilitator. It may well be that a student has identified that they tend to talk about themselves a lot. This isn't a particularly good skill in terms of friendship – if you're talking about yourself you're not listening to or appreciating the perspective of another.

## ACTIVITY 3

### Why Do They Do It?

In this activity the students are asked to consider a series of actions identifying why people do these things and what is their motivation for behaving in this way. They are also asked to clarify how each individual would feel when behaving in this way and to also consider how they themselves would feel if they behaved in this way.

The idea here is to clarify the fact that sometimes we have motivations which may not always be authentic and it is important to try and maintain some level of authenticity in the way in which we approach others and the way in which we act with them and towards them.

## ACTIVITY 4

### Learning to Recognise Others' Social Intelligence

In this activity the students are asked to thought-storm what kind of skills they need if they are to be called a socially intelligent person. These skills might include the following:

- good listening skills
- empathy
- ability to handle one's own emotions

- ability to handle other peoples' emotions
- ability to self-regulate
- ability to keep positive
- ability to maintain motivation
- ability to be authentic.

They are then required to identify a person in the media or other social arena who is particularly famous and socially skilled and successful. What are the skills that they have? They are asked to think about the kinds of skills that they themselves have and whether or not this person also shares such skills or has them in more abundance. It is particularly important to consider the way in which such socially skilled individuals are aware of others' feelings and motives. The students are then asked to identify their top person in terms of this area and to justify their choice, and finally they are asked to consider the ways in which they might like to develop their own skills in this area.

## Plenary

Students can finally focus upon the following questions as part of the plenary discussion:

- What is social intelligence?
- What are the kinds of skills that we need to develop?
- Why is being socially intelligent important?
- How do we know that we are a good friend?
- Why is it important to know our motivations and how these impact upon the ways in which we behave and respond to others?
- Who is the most socially intelligent person and why?
- What are the kinds of skills we need to develop in the future in order to become more socially intelligent?
- Has this session been useful?
- What else could have made the session more helpful? Share ideas.

# SOCIAL INTELLIGENCE: ACTIVITY 1

## How Do They Feel…?

Look at the emotions. Identify the various situations and events that would cause people to feel this way.

| | | |
|---|---|---|
| Thoughtful | Disgusted | Determined |
| Loving | Angry | Shy |
| Hopeful | Caring | Tearful |

List these situations in order of comfort and write your ranking in the box beside each picture. Start with the most comfortable and end with the least comfortable.

Discuss the skills and strategies you think a person should use when they are feeling withdrawn and lonely. What would you suggest?

# SOCIAL INTELLIGENCE: ACTIVITY 2

## My Friendship Skills

People who have good social skills can be good at friendship. Look at the friendship qualities below and rate yourself against each one.

1 = not very often; 3 = quite often; 5 = all the time

| Quality | 1 | 2 | 3 | 4 | 5 |
|---|---|---|---|---|---|
| Show interest in what people do | | | | | |
| Good at giving compliments | | | | | |
| Have a pleasant expression | | | | | |
| Laugh at people's jokes | | | | | |
| Kind | | | | | |
| Ask, not demand, to join in | | | | | |
| Offer to help others | | | | | |
| Invite people to do things | | | | | |
| Hang around where other students are | | | | | |
| Welcoming to other students | | | | | |
| Good at thinking of interesting things to do | | | | | |
| Willing to share | | | | | |
| Humorous and tell jokes | | | | | |
| Fair | | | | | |
| Good at organising games | | | | | |
| Bossy | | | | | |
| Tell others how to behave | | | | | |
| Tell others they are doing things wrong | | | | | |
| Talk about yourself a lot | | | | | |
| Mean what you say | | | | | |
| Talk about other people behind their back | | | | | |
| Negative and sarcastic | | | | | |
| Too intense or serious | | | | | |
| Brag a lot | | | | | |
| Moan a lot | | | | | |
| Bully others | | | | | |
| Claim credit for things you didn't do | | | | | |
| Lie or cheat | | | | | |

Think about three areas you'd like to improve and develop. What do you need to do? Who can help? Discuss with your facilitator.

# SOCIAL INTELLIGENCE: ACTIVITY 3

## Why Do They Do It?

Why do people do these things? What is their motivation? How do they feel? How would you feel if you behaved in this way?

| Action | Motivation | Their feelings | Your feelings |
|---|---|---|---|
| Giving money to charity | | | |
| Stealing from an old person | | | |
| Hitting a sibling | | | |
| Cheating in an exam | | | |
| Shoplifting | | | |
| Helping a friend to complete their work | | | |
| Telling someone that you love them | | | |
| Standing up to bullying | | | |

# SOCIAL INTELLIGENCE: A C T I V I T Y 4

## Learning to Recognise Others' Social Intelligence

Thought-storm! What skills do you need if you are to be called a 'socially intelligent person'?

|  |  |  |
| --- | --- | --- |
|  |  |  |
|  |  |  |
|  |  |  |
|  |  |  |

Now try to think of a famous person you feel is socially skilled and successful. What are their skills? (N.B. Think about the ways they are aware of others' feelings and motives!)

.............................................................................................

.............................................................................................

.............................................................................................

Can you identify your top person in this area and justify your choice?

.............................................................................................

.............................................................................................

.............................................................................................

How would you like to develop your skills?

.............................................................................................

.............................................................................................

.............................................................................................

Discuss with your facilitator.

# Virtue Four

# JUSTICE

## CIVIC STRENGTHS UNDERLIE A HEALTHY COMMUNITY LIFE

# Chapter 13

# FAIRNESS

## TREATING ALL PEOPLE THE SAME ACCORDING TO NOTIONS OF FAIRNESS AND JUSTICE

## Introduction

In this chapter the students are introduced to the concept of fairness and the need to treat everyone the same according to notions of fairness and justice. It is important that as human beings we recognise the importance of social justice and the ways in which people are frequently not treated in the way in which they should be. A quick glance at the television or a read of the newspapers will frequently show us the many times when human beings are not treated fairly or justly and when certain situations cause people to experience a high level of dissonance and anxiety. This is mainly due to the fact that they are not being treated fairly and are not being treated with respect and honesty and not receiving the level of justice that, as human beings, they deserve.

The students are asked to think about whether or not certain situations are fair. Is it fair, for example, that some people are very rich and some people have little or nothing? Is it fair that there are people who are starving in this world? These kinds of big questions are important to consider in our lives as they impact significantly upon the way in which we behave towards other people in our social context.

It is also vital that students are able to identify what is a just response and an unjust response to a range of situations. This is so that they can act accordingly, maintaining a positive, motivated and authentic stance towards others, particularly in difficult or more complex and traumatic situations.

It is also necessary for us, as human beings, to be able to engage in positive reappraisal in difficult times and students are introduced to this concept and have an opportunity to practise these skills. Overall, fairness to self and others is a vital element of maintaining a level of well-being for ourselves and others within the world. We need to know what it is that we have to do in order to maintain a fair, open, honest and authentic pattern of behaviour towards others in this world, and also what they have to do themselves in order to ensure that we feel they are acting in the same way towards us.

# ACTIVITY 1

## Is It Fair?

In this activity the students are asked to stop, think and reflect on a series of statements. These are quite 'big' statements in the sense that some of them concern bigger issues that people are experiencing in the world. For example, some people are very rich and others have nothing and there are many people in this world who are starving. This is not fair, clearly, given the fact that we live in a very rich world, so we need to consider what we in the rich world are doing in order to help and protect and support those who are starving. Students are asked to consider a series of statements in turn and to reflect upon whether or not these are fair and to articulate their own views on each of the scenarios presented.

# ACTIVITY 2

## Recognising a 'Just' Response

This is a key and essential life skill. We need to know what is a just response or an unjust response to a range of situations in our lives and it is important that we develop the kind of reflective skills and stance in order to be able to do this effectively.

The students are presented with a series of situations and are asked to identify when each may be a just response and when it might be an unjust response. It may be the case that bullying a younger child is never a just response but an individual may feel that this is appropriate if that younger child has been bullying someone else. Clearly, such a situation/issue needs to be reflected upon in further detail and with greater depth. For example, is it ever right to bully someone else and why is bullying wrong? This activity probably demands additional time in the sense that there will be some level of debate around each of these scenarios presented.

# ACTIVITY 3

## Positive Reappraisal in Difficult Times

It is evident that when something goes wrong and we may feel upset or hurt we can sometimes cope better if we make use of positive reappraisal. This kind of strategy involves us in attaching a positive meaning to the event, such as identifying what we may have learned from the experience. This strategy is consistent with previous strategies presented and is a key element of maintaining a positive outlook and stance in our lives. The students are asked to try to positively reappraise the problem situation presented. The first one is completed for them in order to give them an idea of this process.

The idea here is for the students to engage with the facilitator or other members of the group in formulating a positive reappraisal of each situation. This reinforces the fact that, even when things seem very difficult and negative, we can by using positive reappraisal find a constructive and positive way forward.

# ACTIVITY 4

## Fairness to Self and Others – My Fairness Rules

It is vital that we know when we are being fair to others and being fair to ourselves. Sometimes we can engage in negative thinking, which can not only tend to reduce our levels of self-esteem but also impact negatively upon our ability to change and move forward. It is, therefore, important to think about the kinds of rules we need for ourselves and for others in order to maintain this kind of level of fairness. For example, I would be fair to myself if I arranged for myself to go regularly to the gym. I'd be fair to myself if I allowed myself some special time to look after my well-being by doing things that I'm interested in and engaging in activities that make me feel good about myself. This activity can be completed and then further reflected upon. Are these rules realistic? Are they rules that would provide and ensure the best outcome both for ourselves and others in our lives?

## Plenary

Students can finally focus upon the following questions as part of the plenary discussion:

- What do we mean by fairness?
- Why is it important to treat all people the same?
- Is it possible to do this or are some people more equal than others?
- What do we mean by justice?
- Why do people need to feel that they are receiving justice particularly when things have gone wrong?
- When are things not fair and when is something not a just response?
- How easy is it to engage in positive reappraisal?
- Do we think that this is a good life skill to develop?
- How can we be fair to ourselves and others?
- Are our fairness rules realistic?
- Has this session been useful?
- What else could have made the session more helpful? Share ideas.

# FAIRNESS: ACTIVITY 1

## Is It Fair?

Stop, think and reflect on these statements; is it fair that:

| | |
|---|---|
| Some people are very rich and others have little or nothing. | One child is clever and another is not. |
| One child has 'good' parents and another doesn't. | Students with special needs are more likely to be bullied. |
| Some parents can buy the 'best' education for their children while others can't. | One person takes the life of another. |
| Not every child has a happy home. | People are starving in this rich world. |
| Some people earn large salaries and don't have to work hard. | Children are used as slave labour in some countries. |
| Some people are 'born beautiful' and others are not. | Some people only have access to slum housing. |

## Recognising a 'Just' Response

What would be a 'just' and an 'unjust' response? Stop, think and reflect and discuss.

| Situation | Just | Unjust |
|---|---|---|
| A student bullying a younger child | | |
| A man who has murdered a child | | |
| A man who physically abuses his wife | | |
| A poor person who shoplifts for food | | |
| A mugger who steals from an old man | | |
| A teacher who bullies a student | | |
| A student who acts up and ruins lessons for others | | |

## FAIRNESS: ACTIVITY 3

## Positive Reappraisal in Difficult Times

When something goes wrong and we feel upset or hurt, we can sometimes cope better if we make use of positive reappraisal. This is when we attach a positive meaning to the event such as identifying what we may have learned from the experience.

Try to positively reappraise the problem situations. The first one is done for you to give you an idea.

| Problem situation | Positive reappraisal |
|---|---|
| Josh did really badly in his exams because he didn't revise enough and now feels stupid and embarrassed. | Josh still has time to revise and now at least he knows what he needs to focus on and can make a proper revision plan. |
| Claire got jealous because her best friend went out with someone else and she felt left out. Her friend thought she was just being silly. | |
| Marcus got detentions every day last week because he was too disorganised and was late for school. He felt angry. | |
| Jane's mum was angry with her because she borrowed her mum's clothes and ripped a hole in her best jumper when she went to a party last Saturday. | |
| Corey wasn't picked for the first team. He wants to be a professional footballer but doesn't see how if they only think he is good enough for the reserves. | |
| Michael felt stupid that he lashed out at the two boys who'd been bullying him as now he'd got a detention. He also didn't think it was fair. | |

## Fairness to Self and Others – My Fairness Rules

| Rules for self | Rules for others |
| --- | --- |
|  |  |

# Chapter 14

# LEADERSHIP

## ORGANISING GROUP ACTIVITIES AND SEEING THAT THEY HAPPEN

## Introduction

In this chapter the students are introduced to the concept of leadership and the ways in which being a good leader can ensure that group activities are organised appropriately and success ensues for all that are involved. The notion of a leader who is positive and can motivate others is also considered. What is it in their language that helps this to be achieved?

The students are asked to think about positive language and motivational language and the way in which it can prompt others into positive actions. They are also asked to consider what actually makes a leader. What are the qualities of someone who can lead others and prompt them into acting authentically and positively within the world and social context?

They are further asked to consider the notions of group responsibility and team membership, identifying their own skills and difficulties in this area prior to engaging in the organisation of a group activity. This involves assigning roles specific to each group and it is important that we recognise what our role is in such tasks and are able to feel secure and confident in filling such roles. Not everybody will feel comfortable in taking on a leading task but they will and should be able to identify key things that they can do in order to make the activity a success and in order to achieve the desired objective.

### ACTIVITY 1

### What is a Leader? Thought-storm

In this activity the students are asked to consider the qualities and nature of leadership. What is it that makes a good leader? What are the kinds of skills, qualities and attributes that this person might need? The student can discuss these with the facilitator or with other members of the group and it may be that certain qualities are more easy to identify than others, for example, a good leader is someone who can motivate and inspire others. However, other qualities may be less obvious. For example, leaders are usually the kinds of people who can manage the emotions and feelings of others really appropriately and ensure that things don't get out of hand and conflicts ensue due to individuals not being able to manage the way that they think, feel and behave.

## ACTIVITY 2

### Leaders Motivate!

In this activity the students are asked to thought-storm the sorts of language that motivate other people. What are the sentences, phrases and tags that they might use, or that they have heard being used, that could be useful in order to motivate others. Ideas can be recorded on the format provided and some examples have been given to prompt thinking. For example, 'Don't give up, you're nearly there. Keep it up!' 'I know you can do it. Go for it!' The idea here is to reinforce the fact that we can all make use of such language; however, it is vitally important that we are authentic in this process and we're not delivering such taglines or phrases simply because we want to manipulate other people into doing things that we want them to do and that they themselves are not very happy to be engaging with.

It is also important to identify this kind of motivational language because there are times when we will need to use this on and for ourselves. We will need to have a series of positive, motivational scripts so that we can ensure that we maintain motivation in our own lives and in our own way of being.

## ACTIVITY 3

### Being a Group Member

In this activity the students can reflect upon their own skills and strengths. What is it that they have that ensures that they perform appropriately as a member of the group? Are they the person who can contribute ideas? Do they have good social skills so that they can engage with those who are finding things difficult? Are they able to identify the strengths of others so that they can use these to promote the success of the group as a whole? What are their difficulties? Do they find it hard to wait and take their turn? Do they find it difficult when others have a diametrically opposed view to their own? Does this cause some emotional dissonance? When reflecting after this activity upon any difficulties it will be important to consider the ways in which these might be addressed. What is it that they could do, think or feel or how could they behave differently in order to ensure that these difficulties are decreased and that they begin to develop more positive skills in terms of being a group member?

## ACTIVITY 4

### Organising a Group Activity – Assigning Roles

In this activity the students are asked to consider a series of roles that they may assign to themselves in a group task. The students are asked to discuss each role in turn with their facilitator or other members of the group and then to consider which role would be the most appropriate for each of them or for themselves. Are there some of these roles that could be swapped?

They are then asked to identify a task that they could complete as part of a group and to assign each member of the group one of these roles. Once the task is complete the students can then discuss how well this went. Who was it that felt most and least comfortable in the role and why? How would they like to operate in the group next time? Would they take on a different role and would this make them feel more comfortable, more productive and more positive? What is important in our lives is that we know where our strengths lie and we know how we can promote and further develop our own self-esteem in terms of taking on roles that are appropriate to our skills base.

## Plenary

Students can finally focus upon the following questions as part of the plenary discussion:

- What have we learnt about leadership?
- What makes a good leader?
- How is it best to organise group activities?
- Does everyone have the same role in the group each time they are engaged in a group activity?
- Can we take on different roles?
- Who are the people who really motivate as leaders and what are the sorts of skills they have?
- Is it possible to further develop our skills as a leader?
- Is everyone meant to be a leader?
- Has this session been useful?
- What else could have made the session more helpful? Share ideas.

## What is a Leader? Thought-storm

What is a LEADER?
Thought- storm!

# LEADERSHIP: ACTIVITY 2

## Leaders Motivate!

Thought-storm! What sort of language motivates others? What sentences, phrases, tags might you use or have heard that could be useful? Record your ideas in the Post-it notes below. Some samples have been provided to prompt your thinking.

Remember! Leaders motivate and use motivational language!

Don't give up, you're nearly there. Keep it up!

I know you can do it. Go for it!

## Being a Group Member

| My strengths | My difficulties |
|---|---|
|  |  |

# LEADERSHIP: ACTIVITY 4

## Organising a Group Activity – Assigning Roles

| | |
|---|---|
| *The Top Ideas Contributor*<br>This person listens to the others in the group and suggests new ideas. They are positive, creative and have lots of energy. | *The Tip Top Researcher*<br>This person seeks information before and during the task to make sure it is clear. They know where and how to share it easily. |
| *The Organised Recorder*<br>This person keeps a record of things that need doing and as they are done. They are organised and good at making notes. | *The Cheerful Encourager*<br>This person praises the ideas of the others and keeps them on track. They are cheerful and positive and make others feel motivated. |

*The Keen Observer*
This person watches the group and looks carefully at what they are doing and how they are doing it. They are good at standing aside and taking in information.

Discuss each role in turn with your facilitator and then consider which role is the most appropriate for each member of your group and why. Are there some roles that could be swapped?

Next, identify a task that you can complete as part of a group and assign each member one of these roles.

When the task is complete, discuss how well this went. Who felt most and least confident in their role and why?

# Chapter 15

# TEAMWORK

## WORKING WELL AS A MEMBER OF A GROUP OR TEAM

## Introduction

In this chapter the students are engaged in activities which reinforce the concepts of leadership and teamwork as in Chapter 14. The idea here is to further identify the kinds of qualities that we need in order to maintain positive roles as members of a team. What is it that makes us a good team player and how can we further develop our skills in this area? This also involves identifying the kinds of rules that we need to adhere to in order to engage in teamwork. What is it that we need to do in terms of working appropriately and skilfully with others and ensuring that their strengths are promoted and their difficulties are catered for?

One of the key qualities of a team player is that they are optimistic. It is therefore a central focus of this chapter that the students are asked to consider their own levels of optimism. Are they optimistic or are they pessimistic and how does being an optimist impact positively upon their ability to interact with others and work successfully as part of a group or team? There is a further opportunity for students to also engage in a team activity whilst also further developing their ability to reflect upon their behaviour in the group. The ability to self-reflect in this way is key and central in terms of further developing skills. We need to know how we functioned and operated as a team member and whether or not we had the kind of positive impact and gave the kind of quality feedback we needed to give in order to ensure that the group was functional and achieved its goals and aspirations.

### ACTIVITY I

#### Qualities of a Good Team Player

In this thought-storm activity the students are asked to identify what the qualities are of someone who is a good team player. What is it that makes everyone want to be on their team? What is it about them? What are the skills/qualities that they have that ensure that the team can work effectively? There are a few examples provided on the format including: this person will be positive and optimistic; they will be able to motivate others; and they can wait their turn in order to listen to others.

It will be useful to identify the range of skills which are appropriate to allocating someone this description and for students then to consider further their own skills in this area. How do they feel about each of these skills and qualities? How do they feel that they could rate themselves against these? It may be useful for students to rate themselves out of 10 as to how they feel they meet each of these key elements and then to consider how they might further develop their skills.

## ACTIVITY 2

### The Optimism Quiz

In this activity the students are asked to consider whether or not they are an optimist or generally a pessimist. This is important when considering our roles within a team. Generally optimists are people who see the cup half full as opposed to half empty. They are the people who can see the solution to the problem and want to engage in problem-solving tasks and activities.

It is therefore important that the students are able to analyse their own skills in this area and also to begin to think how they might further develop and increase their levels of optimism. What is it that they need to do? Do they need to self-nurture more? Do they need to stop negative automatic thoughts and reframe more frequently? Do they need to engage in more positive activities on a daily basis in order to feel better about themselves? This is an opportunity for the students to discuss, either with each other or with the facilitator, the kinds of skills that they need to develop and the behaviours that they need to change in order to remain more optimistic in their lives.

## ACTIVITY 3

### Ten Rules for Teamwork

In this activity the students are asked to identify the key rules that they think would be needed in order to work effectively as a member of the team. These might include listening appropriately, taking turns, being optimistic, remaining motivated, being a good problem solver, finding solutions, able to promote others' strengths and not feel insecure, maintaining good levels of self-esteem.

## ACTIVITY 4

### A Team Challenge – Plan and Evaluate

In this activity the students are asked to identify and agree a team task and to clarify roles for each member of the group. These roles can be consistent with activities from the previous chapter or alternatively they may wish to define their own rules in this task. Step 2 asks them to use the format provided in order to reflect upon a) their behaviours within the group, and b) the behaviour of the group as a whole once the task has been completed. This task clearly demands that the facilitator ensures appropriate time and access to resources for the students and that they have a key task identified for them or by them that they can work on in order to undertake this challenge.

What is important here is reinforcing that it is always important to reflect upon our own behaviours. Did I, for example, build upon other people's ideas in the group or did I put them down? Did I have useful ideas and did I listen appropriately? Did I encourage others and did I give quality feedback to other people in the group? Was I also able to listen to feedback and able to learn from it in the group task? These are key skills that students need to develop and can be reinforced at the end of this activity once students have engaged in the self-reflection activity. This should allow them to identify ways in which they themselves can develop their skills as a group member, and ways in which the group as a whole can further develop in order to work more cooperatively and effectively together.

## Plenary

Students can finally focus upon the following questions as part of the plenary discussion:

- What are the qualities of a good team player?

- Can we agree on these qualities?

- Does a team player have to remain optimistic?

- When would it be right not to be optimistic?

- What sorts of rules are the most important to ensure good teamwork?

- Why is it important to reflect upon our skills as a member of the team?

- What are key skills that we think are totally essential for ensuring productive team activity?

- How can we cope with someone who is not a good team player and finds it difficult?

- What sorts of strategies could we use when someone doesn't exhibit these sorts of skills?

- Has this session been useful?

- What else could have made the session more helpful? Share ideas.

# **TEAMWORK**: ACTIVITY 1

## Qualities of a Good Team Player

Is positive and optimistic

Motivates others

Can wait to listen to others

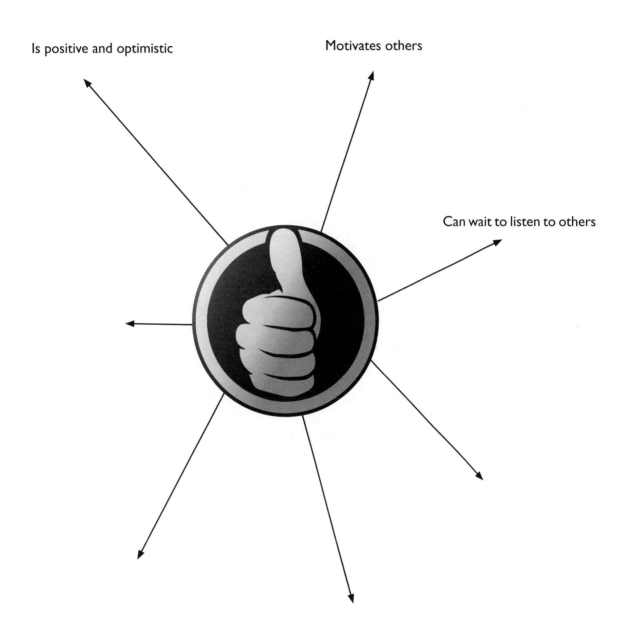

# The Optimism Quiz

Are you an optimist or a pessimist? How would you be likely to respond to the following situations?

Tick against (a), (b), (c) or (d).

You get a low grade in your English exam. Would you think:

a)   I hate English. I'm going to just ignore the work and pretend it doesn't exist.

b)   I'm really disappointed I failed. I must be really stupid.

c)   I should have worked harder. I will from now on.

d)   There must be a mistake! I'm good at English so this result can't be mine.

You have a bad argument with your best friend and totally fall out. Would you think:

a)   That's it! I'm rubbish at friendship. Nobody will ever want me as a friend!

b)   My friend's horrible. I don't want to be friends with him/her anymore anyway.

c)   I expect we'll make up later. I'll keep trying to sort it out.

d)   I'm not bothered! I'll make new friends.

You came last in the race and lost your team ten points. Would you think:

a)   I am such an idiot. Nobody will like me now.

b)   I'm so unlucky. I will never run in a race again.

c)   That was unlucky. I usually run faster than that. I had better practise.

d)   Oh well, at least I had a go!

Your friend says he will invite you to a party on Saturday night but he doesn't. Would you think:

a)   Typical. As usual, he left me out! He always does!

b)   He is just horrible and insensitive!

c)   I don't understand it because he usually does what he says and doesn't let me down.

d)   He must have cancelled the party or something.

Reflect on your responses:

•   Lots of (a) and (b) answers suggest you may be a bit of a pessimist. What can you do in order to change this? Who else can support you? Discuss your ideas with your facilitator.

•   Lots of (c) and (d) answers suggest that you are probably more of an optimist. Why do you think it might be beneficial to be an optimist? How can you increase your level of optimism still further?

## Ten Rules for Teamwork

| 1. |
|----|
| 2. |
| 3. |
| 4. |
| 5. |
| 6. |
| 7. |
| 8. |
| 9. |
| 10. |

# A Team Challenge – Plan and Evaluate

Step 1 – Identify and agree a team task and clarify roles for each member of the group.

...........................................................................

...........................................................................

Step 2 – Use the format below to reflect upon:

1.  your behaviour within the group, and

2.  the behaviour of the group as a whole.

| My behaviour in group | Fully disagree | Partly disagree | Not sure | Partly agree | Fully agree |
|---|---|---|---|---|---|
| I built on the ideas of other people in the group. | | | | | |
| I had some useful ideas. | | | | | |
| I listened to the other people in the group. | | | | | |
| I was encouraging to other people in the group. | | | | | |
| I gave quality feedback and was able to learn from it. | | | | | |
| **Facts about our group** | **Fully disagree** | **Partly disagree** | **Not sure** | **Partly agree** | **Fully agree** |
| Our group worked well together. | | | | | |
| Our group built on each others' ideas and thoughts. | | | | | |
| We explained our ideas clearly to each other. | | | | | |
| We listened to each other. | | | | | |
| We encouraged each other to share ideas and keep going. | | | | | |
| We gave quality feedback to each other and didn't criticise. | | | | | |

# TEMPERANCE

## STRENGTHS THAT PROTECT AGAINST EXCESS

# Chapter 16

# FORGIVENESS

## FORGIVING THOSE WHO HAVE DONE WRONG

## Introduction

In this chapter the students are introduced to the notion of forgiveness and the importance of being able to let go and forgive others who have done wrong, particularly when the wrongdoing is directed towards themselves.

The students are asked to consider this concept and identify what is actually meant by the term forgiveness. Who is it that needs it? What does it involve? What does it mean and why does it matter so much to us as human beings? The idea here is to reinforce the fact that sometimes holding onto anger and pain and other destructive emotions associated with difficult acts is not particularly healthy. We need to learn to look back, re-evaluate the situation and reflect upon it further so that we can identify a way forward. There will be times in our lives where we just need to move on from a certain situation in order to protect our own emotional and mental well-being.

In this chapter the students are also further asked to consider how we can maintain a positive, kind and respectful stance even in the face of difficulties and this involves engaging in the mediation process. It is particularly important to learn skills of mediation in order to cope appropriately with difficult situations that we may be experiencing in the future. There is also an element here of being able to move forward once the damage has been done. Sometimes it is hard to forgive, particularly when an individual may have been very damaged or hurt by someone or a particular event. The importance of being able to leave this behind, metaphorically speaking, cannot be overestimated. Holding onto the feelings associated with such damage can only be harmful in the longer term.

It is also important for us as human beings to be able to forgive ourselves when we have done wrong. This isn't always particularly easy. We tend to look at our mistakes and can get into a negative pattern and cycle of not being able to forgive ourselves for acting stupidly or doing the wrong thing. It is important that we consider what we've actually learnt from such mistakes in order to identify what we could do differently in future situations. Letting go is essential, and as human beings we need to be able to develop our own letting-go scripts in order to maintain and further foster our well-being.

## ACTIVITY I

### What is Forgiveness?

In this activity the students are asked to consider what forgiveness actually is. What is the nature of forgiveness? Who needs it and why do they need it? What is it that we do when we forgive someone? What kinds of acts do we perform and what do we do in terms of addressing the feelings that we have towards them? Does forgiveness actually mean that we forget the act that they've perpetrated or the wrong that they may have done to us or does forgiveness mean that we do actually have to forget that action and move onwards from it? Can we forgive and not forget? These are all pertinent questions that may be useful to cover in this part of the session.

## ACTIVITY 2

### Mediation Process

This activity provides students with an outline of the mediation process. It is particularly important that they begin to develop an awareness of how they can develop these skills. Mediation is an extremely useful process, in which students can actually come to pertinent and appropriate solutions to problems that they are experiencing. The five-step process is as follows:

- Step 1 The mediator agrees not to take sides. The mediator agrees not to offer any solutions. The students agree to speak one at a time and not interrupt each other. They agree to show respect. No blaming or accusations.

- Step 2 The mediator asks each student in turn to describe the problem and how they feel without interrupting each other. The mediator summarises what each one says.

- Step 3 The mediator asks each student to describe how the other one feels.

- Step 4 The mediator asks each student for suggestions regarding 'How can we sort it out?'

- Step 5 The mediator asks the students to agree a solution.

The students are asked to work in groups of three in order to use this five-step process and to act out mediations to a range of problems. Six problems are posed on the activity sheet. It may be that students wish to focus upon three of these in the first instance, so that everyone in the group can take on the role of mediator.

It will then be useful to consider what they have learnt from this experience. How easy was it to be the mediator, and did the process of mediation impact upon the two students who were having the disagreement? Was it easier to resolve this because of the role of the mediator? Did this mean that they could actually describe how they felt and agree a solution without too many problems or difficulties?

## ACTIVITY 3

### Moving Forwards – When the Damage is Done

In this activity the students are asked to consider the times when it can be harder to forgive people. This is when an individual may have been very damaged or hurt by someone's behaviours or actions and this cannot be addressed through the mediation process described earlier.

The students are asked to look at four situations in turn and consider whether or not it would be possible for an individual to forgive the perpetrator in each of these circumstances; if so, why they think this would be possible. They should then consider whether or not they could move on from this in terms of actually leaving their pain and anger behind and how they might be able to do this. This is a particularly difficult activity to undertake as it involves students in really empathising and putting themselves in someone else's shoes. However, what is important is to emphasise the fact that they will have an instinctive reaction to each of these situations and they need to be authentic in actually saying what this is.

## ACTIVITY 4

### Forgive Yourself!

This activity encourages students to think about times when they may have found it difficult to forgive themselves for certain behaviours or actions that they have undertaken. Sometimes it is difficult to forgive ourselves for mistakes we've made. This is a problem, as it can make us feel angry, resentful and ultimately unwell, particularly if we are constantly dwelling on our mistakes and revisiting them in a negative cycle or pattern of thinking. The best thing that we can do in such circumstances is to attempt to reframe the error or mistake by trying to learn from it. Look into the future and how we might act differently next time such a situation occurs.

This activity, therefore, gives students the opportunity to identify a mistake, to articulate the feelings associated with it and the effect that it had upon both themselves and others. They then are required to identify what they could learn from this situation. This is key and central. In order to remain positive and focused, and not to dwell on mistakes we need to identify specifically what it is that we could learn from them. Mistakes are the things that help us to learn; they are the things that help us to change our patterns of behaviour and are an essential part of our lives. We cannot go through our lives without making mistakes but it is how we respond to them that makes all the difference. If we respond in a positive and constructive manner and we actually identify key learning goals from these mistakes then we are protecting ourselves and our future ability to maintain our well-being.

Finally, students are required to formulate letting-go scripts. What is it that I could say to myself in order to let go of the anger and pain I've felt from making such a mistake?

## Plenary

Students can finally focus upon the following questions as part of the plenary discussion:

- What have we learnt about the nature of forgiveness in this session?
- Is mediation an easy process to use?
- Why would mediation be appropriate in many situations?
- Is it easy to take on the role of the mediator?
- Can we always forgive?
- When do we need to simply forget and move onwards?
- Why is it important that we learn how to reframe our mistakes and identify key learning points for ourselves from them?
- Has this session been useful?
- What else could have made the session more helpful? Share ideas.

## What is Forgiveness?

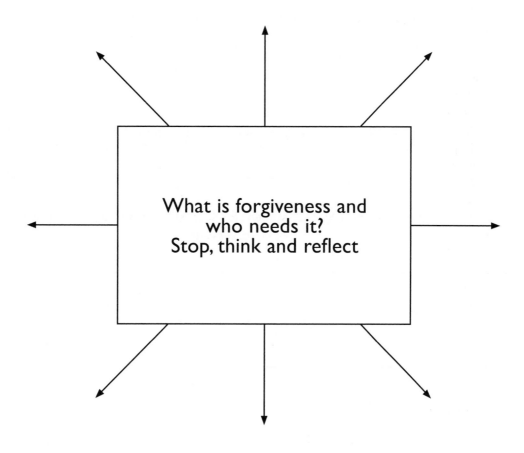

What is forgiveness and
who needs it?
Stop, think and reflect

# FORGIVENESS: ACTIVITY 2

## Mediation Process

| Step 1 | The mediator agrees not to take sides. The mediator agrees not to offer any solutions. The students agree to speak one at a time and not interrupt each other. They agree to show respect. No blaming or accusations. |
|---|---|
| Step 2 | The mediator asks each student in turn to describe the problem and how they feel without interrupting each other. The mediator summarises what each one says. |
| Step 3 | The mediator asks each student to describe how the other one feels. |
| Step 4 | The mediator asks each student for suggestions regarding 'How can we sort it out?' |
| Step 5 | The mediator asks the students to agree a solution. |

Work in threes and use the five-step process to 'act out' mediations for the following six problems:

| | |
|---|---|
| 1. Friends falling out over borrowed clothes – one friend has not returned the items and has ruined one of them. | 2. One person feels left out when he isn't invited to his friend's party because he gets bad-tempered when he drinks. |
| 3. One friend has a new boyfriend/girlfriend and doesn't have time for his/her 'old' friend. | 4. One person has been bullying his/her friend because of jealousy of the way he/she looks and dresses. |
| 5. Friends falling out over money – one friend is always broke and forever borrowing money and not paying it back. | 6. Friends falling out over drugs. One person likes to use cannabis and the other person thinks it's stupid and will result in paranoid behaviour. |

## Moving Forwards – When the Damage is Done

Sometimes it can be harder to forgive than at other times. This is when an individual may have been very damaged or hurt by someone's behaviours/actions and this cannot be addressed through the mediation process. Look at the situations below and think about this – would it be possible for the individual to forgive? Is the damage too great? If so, how can they move on with their lives? What ADVICE would you give?

| | Can they forgive? Why? | Can they 'move on'? How? |
|---|---|---|
| A father whose child has been murdered by a paedophile | | |
| A black woman whose husband has been murdered by a white supremacist | | |
| A young girl who has been raped by her father | | |
| A wife whose husband is continually unfaithful to her | | |

# Forgive Yourself!

Sometimes we can find it difficult to forgive ourselves for the mistakes that we have made. This is a problem as it can make us feel angry, resentful and unwell – particularly if we constantly dwell on our mistakes. The best thing is to reframe the error/mistake by trying to learn from it, looking to the future and how we might act differently next time.

My mistake

......................................................................................................

......................................................................................................

My feelings

......................................................................................................

......................................................................................................

The effect on self and others

......................................................................................................

......................................................................................................

What I could learn from this

......................................................................................................

......................................................................................................

What I would do differently next time

......................................................................................................

......................................................................................................

My 'letting go' script

......................................................................................................

......................................................................................................

# Chapter 17

# MODESTY

## LETTING ONE'S ACCOMPLISHMENTS SPEAK FOR THEMSELVES

## Introduction

In this chapter the students are introduced to the concept of modesty. What does it mean to be modest and why is it so important? Being modest does not equate to having low levels of self-esteem. It is vital that we let our accomplishments speak for themselves and that we do not feel the need to push ourselves forward at the cost of or detriment to others.

In this session the students are introduced again to the concept of self-esteem and the fact that this clearly impacts upon our ability to function appropriately in the social context. We need to feel good about ourselves and have a reasonable level of self-esteem in order to function appropriately. However, we should not be overly self-confident, pompous or bumptious in terms of how we present ourselves to others. This, in effect, could be described as having too high self-esteem or a self-esteem which is unrelated to reality and being inauthentic in an authentic social context.

It is also important that we become increasingly reflective upon and aware of how others' behaviours towards us can impact on our levels of self-esteem and the way that we feel about ourselves and our abilities. People can have decried our particular accomplishments or skills or personal traits in the past and this can have had a negative impact. However, we can also have had experiences when people have encouraged us not to act in a modest way and to present as somewhat full of ourselves; this can also be detrimental, particularly when there is no consistency with such a view and the reality of the situation. It is also necessary to consider when modesty is a virtue and when this could be misconstrued as false modesty. There is a need for us to act with authenticity and assertively within the social context in order to present ourselves as secure and socially skilled human beings. We can be quietly excellent and we can excel at things without being boastful and without putting down others or making them feel insecure because their achievements or accomplishments are not as high or as fast as our own. This is particularly important if we are to maintain positive relationships and be supportive of others within our social frame of reference.

## ACTIVITY 1

### Self-esteem – Low or High?

In this activity the students are presented with a self-esteem assessment. This asks them to consider a series of statements set out under two sections, ticking the boxes that most appropriately fit their own perceptions of themselves. It is not a particularly scientific framework; rather, the idea is to prompt thinking around this area and the activity is set out as typical of one you would find in a teenager's magazine and is therefore intended to have some element of fun.

What is important, however, is that students can think about their levels of self-esteem and just take a broad measure of how they feel about themselves at this current point in time. This then gives the facilitator the opportunity to discuss with them how they might build upon their current levels of self-esteem and improve their skills in terms of maintaining a positive outlook and feelings about themselves as a whole.

## ACTIVITY 2

### What Do People Say?

In this activity the students are encouraged to consider how what people can say to us can affect our self-esteem in both negative and positive ways. What they say can have a real impact upon our feelings and the way that we operate in the social context.

Students are asked to try to identify something that people have said to them about themselves and how this has made them feel. The important thing about this activity is to reinforce the fact that we do not always have to listen to what people say. Sometimes they will be saying things because they feel angry at themselves or they are jealous or they are anxious about something. They will not necessarily be telling us the truth or what we really need to know.

We need to be very careful in terms of not misinterpreting this and actually really understanding their motivations and where they are coming from. This allows us to then evaluate what someone has said and to reject it when we know that it is irrational or inappropriate. For example, if a teacher has lost her temper and then says, 'You always do this in my class', we know that that is not the case because we don't always – she's saying that merely through anger. It isn't something that she would then place on us as a label forever in terms of describing us to other people within that learning context.

## ACTIVITY 3

### When is Modesty a Virtue?

This is a reflection activity in which students focus specifically upon the concept of modesty, identifying times when it would be right or wrong to act in this way. They are also asked to consider whether it is possible for someone to be too modest, and if so how this might affect them and others that they come into contact with. Students can self-reflect upon their own behaviours, and this is an opportunity to really consider whether or not being modest is something that fits with them in an authentic way and whether there is any dissonance between being modest and their behaviours or feelings about themselves. Is this something that they value? Do they think it is a virtue? Is it something that they should develop further as a way of being and behaving or, alternatively, have they been too modest and therefore passive in the past and not asserted themselves or displayed their skills in a quietly assertive manner?

## ACTIVITY 4

### I Can Be Quietly Excellent

This is a key skill. The idea here is to reinforce the fact that we can be quietly excellent. This doesn't necessarily mean that we have to take a back seat or that we have to decry our abilities, but it means that we can show what we can do and do it very, very well without being boastful about it or, in effect, putting others down because they have fewer skills in these particular areas than we do. Students can identify their own skills and talents and accomplishments and then consider specifically how they can let each of these speak for themselves. What is it that they can do and say in order to achieve this without being boastful and maintaining an assertively modest stance?

## Plenary

Students can finally focus upon the following questions as part of the plenary discussion:

- What do we feel about being modest?
- Is this a quality or form of behaviour that we should aspire to?
- Can we have a positive level of self-esteem and not be boastful?
- What does having really good self-esteem mean for us in terms of our behaviour and relationships?
- How have other people impacted upon our self-esteem?
- When would modesty not be a virtue?
- Is there ever a time when we need to boast or be more full of ourselves?
- What do we mean by being quietly excellent?
- Is this something that's easy to achieve?
- How can we achieve it?
- Has this session been useful?
- What else could have made the session more helpful? Share ideas.

# Self-esteem – Low or High?

Answer the following questions and use this code:

Tick box A = Never

Tick box B = Sometimes

Tick box C = Often

Tick box D = Always

## Section 1

| | A | B | C | D |
|---|---|---|---|---|
| Do you think that others like you? | ☐ | ☐ | ☐ | ☐ |
| Do you feel that you have 'good' friends? | ☐ | ☐ | ☐ | ☐ |
| Do you feel that you have good relationships at home? | ☐ | ☐ | ☐ | ☐ |
| Do you feel nervous when asked to start a new topic in a particular subject? | ☐ | ☐ | ☐ | ☐ |
| Can you admit to making mistakes? | ☐ | ☐ | ☐ | ☐ |
| Do you think that you are a capable sort of student, i.e. are you okay at most things? | ☐ | ☐ | ☐ | ☐ |
| Do you trust most people? | ☐ | ☐ | ☐ | ☐ |
| Can you relax and enjoy yourself? | ☐ | ☐ | ☐ | ☐ |
| Do you feel happy in your life? | ☐ | ☐ | ☐ | ☐ |

Section 1 – Now add up your score

A = 1 point

B = 2 points

C = 3 points

D = 4 points          Total = ................

## Section 2

| | A | B | C | D |
|---|---|---|---|---|
| Do you feel miserable if others criticise you? | ☐ | ☐ | ☐ | ☐ |
| Do you feel jealous of other people and their lives? | ☐ | ☐ | ☐ | ☐ |
| Do you worry about what other people think about you? | ☐ | ☐ | ☐ | ☐ |
| Do you think that you need to impress others by the way you look? | ☐ | ☐ | ☐ | ☐ |
| Do you feel as if others don't understand you? | ☐ | ☐ | ☐ | ☐ |
| Do you find yourself in situations where you feel totally excluded from the group? | ☐ | ☐ | ☐ | ☐ |
| Do you dislike people (without telling anyone about it)? | ☐ | ☐ | ☐ | ☐ |
| Do you tend to keep your problems a secret? | ☐ | ☐ | ☐ | ☐ |
| Do you try and please others all the time? | ☐ | ☐ | ☐ | ☐ |
| Do you 'put yourself down' to others (adults and peers)? | ☐ | ☐ | ☐ | ☐ |

# MODESTY: ACTIVITY I

|  | A | B | C | D |
|---|---|---|---|---|
| Do you feel depressed about your life situation? | ☐ | ☐ | ☐ | ☐ |
| Do you feel that you 'miss out' on the chances others get? | ☐ | ☐ | ☐ | ☐ |
| Do you make excuses for not doing things that you know you'd really like to do? | ☐ | ☐ | ☐ | ☐ |
| Do you ever feel that your life is hopeless? | ☐ | ☐ | ☐ | ☐ |
| Do you feel that other people have better relationships than you? | ☐ | ☐ | ☐ | ☐ |
| Do you think that you have to try and impress others with the way you act and behave at school? | ☐ | ☐ | ☐ | ☐ |
| Do you feel shy or awkward in some situations? | ☐ | ☐ | ☐ | ☐ |
| Do you feel 'fed up' at the end of each day? | ☐ | ☐ | ☐ | ☐ |

Section 2 – Now add up your score

A = 4 points

B = 3 points

C = 2 points

D = 1 point          Total = ................

Overall total = ................

## Results – score yourself

### Score 28–43

You need to work on your self-esteem so that you can become a happier and more confident person. START TO THINK POSITIVE: you CAN CHANGE and start to feel good about yourself. You can begin by making small changes to build a better you and to change not just the way you feel about yourself but how you think others feel about you. Make a commitment to being more positive today!

### Score 44–73

Your self-esteem is a bit up and down. You need to start to feel more in control and more confident about your coping strategies. Time to build yourself up and put yourself forward a bit more. Things that may have made you feel a bit fragile before need to be articulated, recognised and swept away. It is time to clean up and shape up, so make a plan!

### Score 74–102

Your self-esteem is okay but you may still lack confidence in a few key areas. These need to be sorted out so that you can become more confident about who you are and start to really recognise and make the most of all those opportunities. Time to build a bit more! Look at those key areas and make a plan!

### Score 103–108

Your self-esteem is fine! Top rating! You are generally positive and feel confident about yourself and your life. Set yourself some new goals – make them bigger and better and aim for the stars!

# What Do People Say?

People can affect our self-esteem in both negative and positive ways. What they say can have a real impact upon our feelings. Try to identify something that each of the following people have said about you and how they made you feel.

| Parent/carer | Friend | Teacher |
|---|---|---|
| They said… | They said… | They said… |
| I felt… | I felt… | I felt… |

| Brother/sister/cousin | Myself | Other |
|---|---|---|
| They said… | They said… | They said… |
| I felt… | I felt… | I felt… |

# **MODESTY**: ACTIVITY 3

## When is Modesty a Virtue?

What is 'modesty'?

...............................................................................................

...............................................................................................

...............................................................................................

When do you think it is 'right' to be modest?

...............................................................................................

...............................................................................................

...............................................................................................

When do you think it is 'wrong' to be modest?

...............................................................................................

...............................................................................................

...............................................................................................

Can someone be too modest and, if so, how does this affect them and others they come into contact with?

...............................................................................................

...............................................................................................

...............................................................................................

Is it ever right to pretend to be modest?

...............................................................................................

...............................................................................................

...............................................................................................

When have you felt or behaved in a modest way?

...............................................................................................

...............................................................................................

...............................................................................................

# MODESTY: ACTIVITY 4

## I Can Be Quietly Excellent

I can let my skills, talents and accomplishments speak for themselves!

| Skills, talents and accomplishments | How I let these speak for themselves – what I do and say |
| --- | --- |
|  |  |

# Chapter 18

# PRUDENCE

## BEING CAREFUL ABOUT ONE'S CHOICES – NOT SAYING OR DOING THINGS THAT MIGHT LATER BE REGRETTED

## Introduction

In this chapter the students are introduced to the concept of prudence. The idea here is to reinforce the fact that one should always be careful about the choices that one makes and, particularly, not put oneself in the position of making promises that one cannot keep. Also, being prudent helps us to avoid engaging in activities and reacting in a way that we might later regret. The idea here is to think about the future consequences of our behaviours and to act in an informed manner in whatever we do. We need, as human beings, to be able to identify and distinguish between good and bad choices. For example, is smoking a good choice or is relaxing and looking after oneself and setting appropriate goals a good choice?

The students are introduced to this idea and given the opportunity to consider the choices that they currently make. Also in this chapter there is a focus upon the fact that we can all choose to change. We do not necessarily have to maintain the status quo and keep repeating the kinds of behaviours that we have been engaged in in the past, particularly when these have negative outcomes for both ourselves and others in our social context.

Making good choices is something that we can all learn how to do and we can get better at it. It is another essential life skill. This ability helps us to go through life with fewer regrets than we would have done had we not developed such skills. Engaging in positive actions and doing good things on a daily basis helps us to avoid such situations and the consequent, regretful feelings that we can experience. This is something that we can actually plan for and this needs to be reinforced with students in this particular session.

### ACTIVITY 1

### Good and Bad Choices

In this activity the students are presented with a series of choice cards. These detail a range of activities that they may or may not engage in. The students can engage in discussion with the facilitator, or other members of the group as appropriate, in order to consider the extent to which these are either good or bad choices. What is it that makes a bad choice? Is it the outcomes? Is it the fact that something actually causes harm to both ourselves and others? It is also important to reinforce the fact that we do have a choice here. We can choose to engage in things that are harmful to us and others or we can choose not to. We do not always have to be reliant upon others in our social context to persuade us otherwise.

## ACTIVITY 2

### Choosing to Change

In this activity students are asked to stop, think and reflect upon a relationship that they would like to change currently and why this would be a good choice to make at this point in time. They are required to draw two pictures as follows: the current relationship as it is, using places, objects and other people that are involved in it; and then the relationship as they would like it to be. Once again this is the notion of envisaging a preferred future for a particular aspect of our lives. Students are then asked to consider the following:

- How did they feel when completing each of the drawings?
- What was their motivation for wanting to change the relationship?
- What could they do next in order to reach this goal?

They are required to identify the next three steps. Once again this kind of stepped process to problem solving and personal change is highlighted and reinforced. It is a powerful mechanism for ensuring that we do actually achieve the best possible outcome.

## ACTIVITY 3

### Making Good Choices

In this activity the students are required to identify three good choices that they have made in the past. They can then complete the activity, which requires them to identify why this was a good choice. What would have made it a bad choice and what could they do differently in the same situation next time? (That is, if they had made a reasonable choice but it could have been even better they can identify the key things that they could have done in order to make it so.)

## ACTIVITY 4

### Don't Regret Diary!

This is a planning ahead activity. The students are asked to record a) something they could think, b) something they could say, and c) something that they could do for each day of the week. They are required to identify things that they know they would not regret and would produce a positive outcome both for themselves and others. Keeping such a diary can reinforce not only the positives but also the fact that students do have the ability to take action and to engage in activities and behaviours that will produce positive outcomes. This is particularly powerful. We do not have to regret everything that we do, particularly if we consider what we were doing beforehand and opt to make appropriately good and positive choices in our lives.

## Plenary

Students can finally focus upon the following questions as part of the plenary discussion:

- What do we mean when we refer to prudence?
- How can we be sure that we are making the right choices in our lives?

- Why is it important to avoid regrets?
- Why is it important to learn from bad choices that we have made?
- How can we best do this?
- Is it important not to dwell on our mistakes and feel regretful? If so, why?
- Has this session been useful?
- What else could have made the session more helpful? Share ideas.

## Good and Bad Choices

| | | |
|---|---|---|
| Smoking | Telling the truth | Taking time to self-nurture |
| Keeping fit | Talking others down | Over-eating |
| Taking drugs | Working hard | Relaxing |
| Cheating in assessments | Being negative | Self-harming |
| Being sexually promiscuous | Going to the gym | Setting goals |

## Choosing to Change

Stop, think and reflect! Think of a relationship you would like to change and why this would be a good choice to make. Draw the following two pictures:

| Picture 1 | Picture 2 |
|---|---|
| Illustrate the relationship as it is at present by using places, objects and other people that are involved in it: | Illustrate the relationship as you would like it to be: |
|  |  |

1. How did you feel when completing each of the drawings?
2. What is your motivation for wanting to change the relationship?
3. What can you do next in order to reach this goal? Identify the next three steps.

1) ...................................................................................................

...................................................................................................

...................................................................................................

2) ...................................................................................................

...................................................................................................

...................................................................................................

3) ...................................................................................................

...................................................................................................

...................................................................................................

## Making Good Choices

Think of three 'good' choices you have made in the past! Then complete the activity as follows:

| | **Why was this a good choice?** | **What would have made this a 'bad' choice?** | **Would I do anything differently in the same situation next time?** |
|---|---|---|---|
| Choice 1 | | | |
| Choice 2 | | | |
| Choice 3 | | | |

# **PRUDENCE**: ACTIVITY 4

## Don't Regret Diary!

Plan ahead! Record:

1.  something you can think

2.  something you can say

3.  something you can do

for each day of the week that you KNOW you will not regret and that will produce a positive outcome for you and others.

|  | **Think** | **Say** | **Do** |
|---|---|---|---|
| Monday | | | |
| Tuesday | | | |
| Wednesday | | | |
| Thursday | | | |
| Friday | | | |
| Saturday | | | |
| Sunday | | | |

# Chapter 19

# SELF-REGULATION

## REGULATING WHAT ONE FEELS AND DOES

## Introduction

In this chapter the students are introduced to the concept of self-regulation. This is hugely important in our lives. We need to be able to know how we're feeling, why we're feeling it and to be able to choose to make alternative responses if these are going to achieve a better outcome for ourselves. This is essentially about managing our emotions, our feelings, thoughts and behaviours, and we need to be able to distinguish between these and consider how the way in which we think impacts on the way we feel and what we do. However, within this process there is a choice once again to be made – we can choose to respond differently to the thoughts and feelings that we have, particularly when we know that the way in which we behaved previously has not achieved the best outcome for ourselves and others.

It is also important that students are able to distinguish between comfortable and uncomfortable feelings and have the ability, skills and strategies to actually manage those feelings which are uncomfortable and cause them higher levels of stress and anxiety. Developing the ability to manage stress and anger is clearly a crucial life skill and one which is focused upon in this chapter.

### ACTIVITY 1

### How Do I Think, Feel and Do? Cognitive Behaviour Approach

In this activity the students are introduced to the cycle of thinking, feeling and behaving, in the context of a series of examples. The students are then asked to consider the statement, 'How you will think about something will become true.' Is this really the case?

From a cognitive behaviour therapy perspective this is indeed the case. Generally if we tend to think about something in a negative way we will respond to something in a negative way and it will become a self-fulfilling prophecy. It is important to develop the skill of stopping ourselves at the point of thinking. We think something and then we need to check it out. Is it true? For example, I might think that I'm useless at a certain task – is this true? I need to check it out with friends, relatives, other people who have observed me engaged in this task. They may well give me different feedback to the feedback that I'm giving myself. If I give myself the negative feedback that I'm useless then I will feel dreadful and I will then repeat the kind of negative behaviour that I've been previously engaged in.

Students are asked to think about this statement. Is it true? Can we change the way we think? Can we handle our problems differently to change how we feel and what we do? Can we gain more control over what happens to us in our lives? Clearly the idea here is to present the students with the fact that of course we can do this and it's merely a matter of beginning to engage in the kinds of positive behaviour change and ways of thinking that will ensure that we can prevent ourselves from falling into the same traps again and again in terms of how we behave in and respond to certain situations.

## ACTIVITY 2

### When Feelings are Comfortable and Uncomfortable

Clearly this is a distinction that we all need to be able to make. We need to be aware of how we feel but also of the way in which these feelings impact upon our behaviours. There are feelings that we have that are particularly comfortable, for example when we are feeling happy, content and relaxed. There are others that are generally uncomfortable, for example when we feel angry or stressed or tense. However, there are others that may be a mixture of both. For example, feeling excited might be both comfortable and uncomfortable; it may have pleasurable aspects but it may also engender a certain level of stress.

Students are asked to stop, think and reflect as to why it is unhelpful to label feelings as being good or bad. This is particularly important; for example, being angry is not necessarily bad and being fearful is not necessarily bad. We need to feel angry when things are unjust and wrong and we need to show that anger in an assertive, calm and authentic manner. If someone is being racist towards somebody else and it is unjustified, unnecessary and inappropriate then we should rightly feel angry and we should be able to express this anger in an appropriately calm and assertive fashion.

## ACTIVITY 3

### Anger Management Strategies

This information sheet introduces students to a range of anger management strategies that they may be able to utilise in order to cope more effectively with angry situations.

Students are asked to consider which one or more of the strategies they might like to use or find appropriate in order to manage their behaviour more effectively. They can also identify their own personal strategy that they may be using to help them in such situations and with such uncomfortable feelings. It is important that the facilitator reinforces the fact that being angry and feeling angry is not necessarily wrong. There are situations in which anger is a useful tool for change and for enabling people, including themselves, to move forward.

## ACTIVITY 4

### Self-management Skills – My Script

In this activity the students are asked to proceed through a traffic light system – stop, wait, reflect – as follows:

**Stop!** What am I feeling? (Check your early warning signs.) What is happening here? (Check your thinking.) Check your 'state'. (Breathe deeply and less quickly.)

**Wait!** What strategies can I use for this situation? What is my contingency plan?

**Reflect!** Respond rather than react. Check your tone of voice and its pitch. Check your gestures and defuse instinctive reactions. Check your proximity. Keep eye contact.

**GO!** What rehearsed words/phrases/statements/techniques shall I use?

They are then required to consider what kind of script they could use at the 'go' stage. What rehearsed words or phrases or statements or techniques could they use in order to then move forward in any difficult or complex situation in which they are feeling angry, stressed or particularly put upon? This is an extremely useful strategy to develop as it helps us to stop reactive responses and engage in more considered approaches, in which we make use of our intellect and ability to think and reflect in order to solve problems that confront us on a daily basis. Ultimately, it is all about the ability to self-regulate what one feels and does in the most constructive manner possible.

## Plenary

Students can finally focus upon the following questions as part of the plenary discussion:

- What do we know about the link between thinking, feeling and behaving?
- How can we stop ourselves from responding to our negative thoughts?
- What is it that we can tell ourselves to do in certain situations in order to avoid falling into the trap of negative responses?
- When are feelings most uncomfortable?
- What kinds of strategies work best for us in terms of managing these uncomfortable feelings?
- Is it important to develop systems to manage complex and uncomfortable feelings?
- What kind of script works best for us?
- Has this session been useful?
- What else could have made the session more helpful? Share ideas.

## How Do I Think, Feel and Do? Cognitive Behaviour Approach

How do the links work?

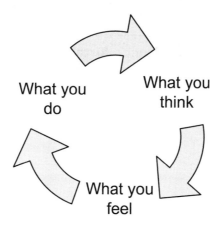

Some examples:

| Think | Feel | Do |
|---|---|---|
| I'm useless at meeting new people. | I feel scared and nervous when I meet new people. | I don't talk to them and go quiet. |
| Nobody in my form likes me. | I feel sad and angry. | I avoid going out at break and start to bunk off school. |
| I'm rubbish at maths. | I feel stupid and fed up. | I stop trying because I know I'll get it wrong. |

Statement: How you think about something will become true.
Stop, think and reflect:

- Is this true?
- Can we change the way we think?
- Can we handle our problems differently to change how we feel and what we do?
- Can we gain more control over what happens to us in our lives?

## When Feelings are Comfortable and Uncomfortable

Thought-storm – identify feelings that are comfortable, uncomfortable and sometimes a mixture of both.

| Comfortable | Uncomfortable | A mixture of both |
|---|---|---|
|  |  |  |

Stop, think and reflect – why is it unhelpful to label feelings as being 'good' or 'bad'? For example, is anger always a 'bad' thing?

**SELF-REGULATION**: ACTIVITY 3

# Anger Management Strategies

Which strategies might you use to cope more effectively? Can you think of others?

| | | |
|---|---|---|
| *Deep breathing whilst counting backwards*<br>Breathe in through nose.<br>Breathe out through your mouth saying 'ten'.<br>Repeat saying 'nine'.<br>Continue through to 'zero'. | *Catchphrase*<br>Come up with a particular phrase to say to yourself for when you get angry. Practise saying it so you are ready to use it when you do get angry. | *Counting to ten*<br>When you begin to feel angry, do not let yourself react until you have counted to ten. |
| *Talk sense to yourself*<br>Become aware when you start to get angry.<br>Talk yourself through the anger by saying things like:<br>'I am going to be ok.'<br>'Just stay calm.'<br>'It will be over soon.'<br>'It's not worth it.' | *Deep breathing*<br>Breathe in through the mouth slowly, imagining your tummy as a balloon filling up with air. Breathe in until you have no space left.<br>Slowly let all the air out until there is nothing left inside you. | *Deep breathing whilst thinking positive thoughts*<br>Close your eyes.<br>Breathe deeply through your nose.<br>Breathe out through your mouth and think of a positive thought.<br>Describe the picture in your mind to yourself, commenting on the smells, colours, sounds and so on. |
| *Stop, think, act*<br>When you are in a difficult situation stop, think, act. | *Breathing control*<br>Breathe in through your nose.<br>Breathe out through your mouth.<br>Say a word to yourself each time, such as 'calm' or 'peace'. | *Reflecting*<br>After an incident think back to events. Talk through the situation, changing key actions, trying to achieve a better outcome. |
| *Time-out*<br>Ask for a time-out card at school and work out a plan with the teacher as to where you would go if you needed to use it. | *Stop negative thoughts*<br>Practise thinking negative thoughts.<br>When someone says 'stop', turn them into positive ones. | *Other* |

## Self-management Skills – My Script

**Stop!** What am I feeling? (Check your early warning signs.) What is happening here? (Check your thinking.) Check your 'state'. (Breathe deeply and less quickly.)

**Wait!** What strategies can I use for this situation? What is my contingency plan?

**Reflect!** Respond rather than react. Check your tone of voice and its pitch. Check your gestures and defuse instinctive reactions. Check your proximity. Keep eye contact.

**GO!** What rehearsed words/phrases/statements/techniques shall I use?

| Write your script here |
| --- |
| |

# TRANSCENDENCE

## STRENGTHS THAT FORGE CONNECTIONS TO THE LARGER UNIVERSE AND PROVIDE MEANING

# Chapter 20

# APPRECIATION OF
# BEAUTY AND EXCELLENCE

## NOTICING AND APPRECIATING BEAUTY, EXCELLENCE AND/OR SKILLS PERFORMANCE IN ALL DOMAINS OF LIFE

## Introduction

In this chapter students are presented with the concepts of beauty and excellence and why it is particularly important for them to appreciate these. As human beings we need, on a frequent basis, to notice and appreciate what is beautiful and excellent in the world. This isn't always easy, particularly if we are engaged in negative cycles and patterns of behaviour and we are feeling particularly down at any one point in our lives. However, looking at what is going well, looking at what works well, looking at what is excellent and lovely in the world, can certainly help us and refresh us in terms of making us more positive and more able to maintain motivation.

In this session the students are asked to consider the nature of beauty and excellence and also to identify their own skills and qualities. What is it that makes them excellent? What is it that makes them beautiful? This can be quite difficult for some individuals; however, it is important for the facilitator to reinforce the fact that this is an essential skill. We need to be able to do this in order to maintain our own levels of self-esteem and also to be able to react and respond positively in the world to others.

Students also have the opportunity to consider and appreciate the excellence and special nature of others' contributions and abilities. The things that they do that impact upon them that make a real difference. Noticing the best is a key skill in our lives. It is very easy for people to go through each day noticing everything that is wrong, everything that is bad and everything that is negative. Making comments from the moment we wake up ('Oh, isn't the weather bad', 'Oh, I've missed the bus') is not always helpful. At the end of a day like this you will tend to feel extremely down and extremely negative. It is much more helpful to be able to get up in the morning and say, 'The weather's not that good but look at this..., look at that lovely bit of blue sky up there..., look at the wonderful trees in my drive', and look and appreciate all that is around you.

There will also be good acts that we observe in others. Not everything that people do is bad or manipulative. We will be able to observe people doing kind acts on a daily basis as long as we are in a mindset to be able to do this. We need to be actively looking for it and then we will notice it.

## ACTIVITY 1

### What is Beauty? What is Excellence?

In this activity the students are asked to define beauty and excellence. What is it that makes something beautiful? Is beauty actually the same for all people or can we see beauty in different things and have different perspectives on this? This is important. People often say that 'beauty is in the eye of the beholder' and sometimes when we love somebody we think they are beautiful even though others might not share our viewpoint. This is absolutely fine. It is a key aspect of our relationships with others that we identify the beauty and the wonderful aspects that we perceive in other people and we value and treasure them.

## ACTIVITY 2

### My Excellent Skills and Qualities

In this activity the students can work with the facilitator or other members of the group in order to identify their own skills and qualities. What is it that they do? What is it that they have in terms of qualities that makes them excellent and makes them present themselves in the world as authentic, positive, motivated and decent individuals? These are the qualities that we all should be aspiring to. These are the qualities and skills that, if we develop them, will essentially ensure our well-being throughout our lives and also impact positively on all our relationships with others.

## ACTIVITY 3

### Appreciating the Excellence and Special Nature of Others

In this activity students are asked to identify four individuals who exhibit excellence in some way and all of whom are special to them. They are then asked to try to identify the key qualities that these individuals have and the impact upon themselves. This is particularly important as it is necessary for us to continually recognise the wonderful nature of individuals in our lives who love us and support us. This prevents us from taking them for granted but also raises our awareness as to what we should be aspiring to, in terms of our behaviours and responses to others.

## ACTIVITY 4

### Noticing the Best

In this activity the students are required to keep a diary noting down the 'best' things on a daily basis.

This, once again, is a useful strategy for young people to begin to develop at the earliest opportunity. Regarding what is the best and looking for the positives in life is clearly key – an essential in terms of keeping us positive ourselves. If we can develop this essential skill then we are far less likely to engage in negative thought patterns and negative automatic thoughts which then generally lead to us feeling depressed and down. The idea here is to reinforce the fact that this simple technique can most certainly enable us to feel and remain positive every day of the week.

## Plenary

Students can finally focus upon the following questions as part of the plenary discussion:

- How do we define beauty and how do we define excellence?
- Why is it important to notice when people exhibit such qualities or when a situation is one of excellence and beauty?
- How does it make us feel when we continually notice what is beautiful and excellent?
- When might this be a problem?
- When might it be difficult to notice what is beautiful and excellent?
- What could we do in such a situation in order to maintain a positive stance?
- Why is noticing the best a good and essential life skill for us all to develop?
- Has this session been useful?
- What else could have made the session more helpful? Share ideas.

## APPRECIATION OF BEAUTY AND EXCELLENCE: ACTIVITY 1

### What is Beauty? What is Excellence?

| Beauty | Excellence |
| --- | --- |
|  |  |

## My Excellent Skills and Qualities

| Skills | Qualities |
| --- | --- |
|  |  |

## Appreciating the Excellence and Special Nature of Others

Identify four individuals who exhibit excellence in some way and are special to you. Then try to identify their key qualities and their impact on you.

| Person 1 | Person 2 |
|---|---|
| Key qualities:<br><br><br><br><br><br>Impact on me: | Key qualities:<br><br><br><br><br><br>Impact on me: |
| **Person 3** | **Person 4** |
| Key qualities:<br><br><br><br><br>Impact on me: | Key qualities:<br><br><br><br><br>Impact on me: |

# APPRECIATION OF BEAUTY AND EXCELLENCE: ACTIVITY 4

## Noticing the Best

Keep a diary – note down these things on a daily basis:

a)   the 'best' kind act you saw

b)   the 'best' kind act you made

c)   the 'best' feeling you had

d)   the 'best' feeling you caused others to experience

e)   the 'best' moment in each day

f)   the 'best' thought you had

| Monday | a)<br>b)<br>c) | d)<br>e)<br>f) |
|---|---|---|
| Tuesday | a)<br>b)<br>c) | d)<br>e)<br>f) |
| Wednesday | a)<br>b)<br>c) | d)<br>e)<br>f) |
| Thursday | a)<br>b)<br>c) | d)<br>e)<br>f) |
| Friday | a)<br>b)<br>c) | d)<br>e)<br>f) |
| Saturday | a)<br>b)<br>c) | d)<br>e)<br>f) |
| Sunday | a)<br>b)<br>c) | d)<br>e)<br>f) |

# Chapter 21

# GRATITUDE

## BEING AWARE OF AND THANKFUL FOR THE GOOD THINGS THAT HAPPEN

## Introduction

In this chapter the students are introduced to the concept of gratitude and why it is vital for us in our lives to be aware of and thankful for the good things that happen to us and the good things that happen to others. The students are initially introduced to the concept of looking for the good. This reinforces the activities in the previous session – that is, looking for what is excellent and beautiful. When we look for what is good on a daily basis it is clearly a healthy option in terms of ensuring that we maintain a positive outlook ourselves.

This chapter asks students to engage in a range of daily, positive psychology activities; reflecting upon and recording a running record of goodness and saying a daily thank you for things that have gone well and things that have been important, lovely and meaningful in their lives. It is important that we show gratitude and that we recognise the good things that are happening to us on a regular, daily basis. This, once again, reinforces the notion of being alive, being full of zest and motivation and maintaining a positive outlook on life as a whole.

### ACTIVITY 1

#### Looking for the Good

In this activity students are asked to record good things that happen to themselves or others during the subsequent week. Good actions or deeds that they observe, that happen at home, and in the wider world in this subsequent week. These are key areas of their circle of life and circle of influence in which good things can have happened. It is important to identify these and to reinforce them, as opposed to dwelling on the negatives, and this kind of strategy will support them in this objective.

### ACTIVITY 2

#### My Goodness Running Record

In this activity the students are asked to keep a daily diary of good deeds that they or others have performed for one whole day. These can be recorded on the format provided and then read through at the end of that day. The students can then reflect upon how this goodness running record makes them feel. Such a running record could also be posted up onto their bedroom wall or somewhere relatively accessible, such as in a diary, and referred to on a continual basis. This is evidence of what happens on a good day. This is evidence that on a daily basis there are many good acts and good and positive outcomes that occur. This needs to be reinforced as reflecting upon what is good in each day helps us to remain positive.

## ACTIVITY 3

### Saying a Daily Thank You

In this activity the students are asked to make a point of saying a daily 'thank you'. This involves recording the names of all the people who are in their lives who help them, love them, show them friendship and are important to them. The students can then make sure that they thank these individuals for what they actually do. This is undertaken for a one-day period. It may be possible for students to then formulate their own thank-you scripts for each individual concerned. How we can show our gratitude to each of these individuals and also reinforce the fact that saying 'thank you' is so important in terms of making others feel good and maintaining both our own and their levels of self-esteem and positive feelings.

## ACTIVITY 4

### Reinforcing the Positive

In this activity the students are asked to think about their positive points and identify these according to their own viewpoint, according to what their friends might say, according to what their family members might say, and according to what teaching staff may say. If they cannot do this independently of feedback from others it may be useful to ask them to take this activity away and go and ask people – that is, collect the appropriate evidence. What is it that their friends would say about them that is positive? Are they kind, generous, good, a good listener, motivated, empathic, sensitive, caring, thoughtful? It is vital that we all can identify our positive points in order to maintain levels of self-esteem but also to maintain a positive outlook on life in general.

## Plenary

Students can finally focus upon the following questions as part of the plenary discussion:

- Why is it important to be aware of the good things that happen to us?
- What happens when we forget to focus upon the good things that happen in our lives?
- Is looking for good a useful strategy?
- Why is keeping a running record of 'thank you's and good deeds so important?
- Do we always need to rely on others to reinforce the positive aspects of our own characters and personalities?
- Can we do this for ourselves alone? If not, why not? If so, how?
- Has this session been useful?
- What else could have made the session more helpful? Share ideas.

# GRATITUDE: ACTIVITY 1

## Looking for the Good

Take note of…

| | |
|---|---|
| Good things that have happened to me/others this week. | Good actions and deeds I have observed this week. |
| Good things that have happened at home this week. | Good things that have happened in the wider world this week. |

## GRATITUDE: ACTIVITY 2

## My Goodness Running Record

Keep a daily tally of good deeds you or others have performed for one whole day. Record these below and then read through them at the end of the day. How does this goodness running record make you feel now?

| Time | Your good deed | Others' good deeds |
|------|----------------|--------------------|
|      |                |                    |

# GRATITUDE: ACTIVITY 3

## Saying a Daily Thank You

Make a point of saying thank you! Record the names of all the people who are in your life who help you, love you, show you friendship, are important to you, etc. Then make sure you thank them for what they do – try it out for a day! Write your 'thank you' scripts.

| Name | My thank you script |
|------|---------------------|
|      |                     |
|      |                     |
|      |                     |
|      |                     |
|      |                     |
|      |                     |
|      |                     |
|      |                     |
|      |                     |
|      |                     |
|      |                     |
|      |                     |

## Reinforcing the Positive

My positive points…

| According to me | According to my friends |
|---|---|
|  |  |

# Chapter 22

# HOPE

## EXPECTING THE BEST
## AND WORKING TO ACHIEVE IT

## Introduction

In this chapter the students are introduced to the concept of hope. What does it mean to be hopeful and to think and expect the best out of life, and how does this impact, particularly on our well-being and the way in which we respond to others? Being hopeful is clearly an essential life skill in terms of remaining positive and being able to work to achieve our goals.

The students are asked to reflect hopefully upon their futures, identifying and visualising their own perfect futures and also the kinds of support systems that they might need in order to be able to achieve such goals. Looking at the way in which our lives might be if a miracle had happened and everything is perfect is often a useful strategy for identifying the changes that we might need to make in order to move further towards that goal. The students are introduced to the solution-focused strategy of talking through a miracle day and then identifying specific targets in order to improve their current sense of well-being and achieve a more positive situation for themselves.

### ACTIVITY 1

#### My Ideal Self – Be Full of Hope!

In this activity the students are asked to visualise their perfect future. Who will they be? What will they be doing, thinking and feeling? Where will they be and who will be with them? Also they are required to identify the skills, qualities and attributes that they would have and the ways in which these would make them this special ideal self. They can record their ideas on the drawing/writing frame provided and discuss these with the facilitator. Why do they want to be this way? Why do they visualise themselves in this way? What is it about being this sort of person and individual and having these kinds of skills and attributes that is so positive?

### ACTIVITY 2

#### My Miracle Day

In this activity the students can complete the diary of their miracle day. What would be happening to them if they had the most wonderful day ever, nothing was wrong and all their problems had disappeared? How would they feel, think and act at each hour of the day? Why would this be so special and positive for them? The students can record their responses next to the time diary entries from 7.00am through to 11.00pm. Once this has been completed they can then stop, think and reflect. How is this miracle day different from their usual day? They can record the differences or articulate these with their facilitator, identifying key aspects of this miracle day that they would like to feel would be in their usual day and the kinds of things that they might have to do in order to move from the normal to the miracle day in the future.

## ACTIVITY 3

### Miracle Day Top Targets

In this activity the students are asked to look back at their miracle day and specifically reflect further upon the differences between this day and their usual day. What is it that they would really like to change about their normal day in order to make it more like the miracle day? What small steps could they do now in order to begin to work towards their idea?

The students are required to complete the chart presented on the activity sheet and share their targets either with a partner or their facilitator. They are also asked to consider how practical and realistic these targets are and to identify any ways in which they might be able to help both themselves and each other in order to stay positive and expect the best.

Reflecting upon how they will know when they've reached their targets is also a vital part of this activity. We need to be able to articulate what it is that will be different once we've reached our goals. Once again this solution-focused process is an extremely important and useful life skill that can be used again and again in order to further promote change and positive well-being.

## ACTIVITY 4

### Supporting Others to Keep Hopeful! 'WWW'

In this activity the students are asked to consider how they can support others in order to help them to keep hopeful and positive and focus upon what went well (WWW). This strategy helps us to counter our in-built negative bias – that is, our tendency to focus on the negative. It helps to make us more successful and healthier in both the short and longer term.

The students are asked to focus on three key 'W' questions: What went well this year? What went well this term? What went well today? They are prompted to ask themselves the WWW questions and to ask them in the future in a range of different contexts and with a range of different people including members of their family, members of their peer group and members of their support system. This strategy, once again, is an extremely useful tool of appreciative enquiry in terms of maintaining a positive outlook and stance on life.

## Plenary

Students can finally focus upon the following questions as part of the plenary discussion:

- Why is it important to have hope in our lives?
- Why would people not have hope in their lives?
- Why do we need to always try to expect the best?
- When is it easier to work towards the best?
- What are the situations and circumstances that make this possible?
- How can we engage in more positive thinking?

- What is the best way to formulate targets for ourselves?

- Why is focusing on what works well important and can we see ourselves using this strategy in the future?

- Has this session been useful?

- What else could have made the session more helpful? Share ideas.

## My Ideal Self – Be Full of Hope!

Visualise your perfect future! Who will you be? What will you be doing, thinking and feeling? Where will you be and who will be with you? What skills, qualities and attributes will you have that will make you this special 'ideal' self? Record your ideas in the frame below.

# HOPE: ACTIVITY 2

## My Miracle Day

Complete this diary of your miracle day. What would be happening to you? How would you feel, think and act at each hour of the day? Why would it be so special and positive?

| Time | Diary entry |
| --- | --- |
| 7.00am | |
| 8.00am | |
| 9.00am | |
| 10.00am | |
| 11.00am | |
| 12.00 noon | |
| 1.00pm | |
| 2.00pm | |
| 3.00pm | |
| 4.00pm | |
| 5.00pm | |
| 6.00pm | |
| 7.00pm | |
| 8.00pm | |
| 9.00pm | |
| 10.00pm | |
| 11.00pm | |

Now stop, think and reflect! How is this different from your usual day? Record the differences below in brief note form/discuss with your facilitator.

Differences from my normal day…

## Miracle Day Top Targets

Look back at your miracle day and the differences between this day and your usual day. What would you really like to change about your normal day in order to make it more like the miracle day? What small steps could you take now in order to begin to work towards your ideal?

Complete the chart below and share your targets with a partner/your facilitator. How practical and realistic are they? Are there any ways you might be able to help each other? How can you stay positive and expect the best?

|  | **What I want it to be like** | **My target – how can I get there?** | **How will I know I have reached my target?** |
|---|---|---|---|
| Difference 1 |  |  |  |
| Difference 2 |  |  |  |
| Difference 3 |  |  |  |

## Supporting Others to Keep Hopeful! 'WWW'

You can support others to keep hopeful and positive by helping them to focus on what went well (WWW)! This strategy helps us to counter our inbuilt negative bias – our tendency to focus on the negative. It helps to make us more successful and healthier.

Ask yourself the WWW questions and ask others in your family, peer group and support system!

What went well this year?

..................................................................................................................

..................................................................................................................

..................................................................................................................

..................................................................................................................

..................................................................................................................

..................................................................................................................

What went well this term?

..................................................................................................................

..................................................................................................................

..................................................................................................................

..................................................................................................................

..................................................................................................................

..................................................................................................................

What went well today?

..................................................................................................................

..................................................................................................................

..................................................................................................................

..................................................................................................................

..................................................................................................................

..................................................................................................................

# Chapter 23

# HUMOUR

## LIKELY TO LAUGH AND TEASE; BRINGING SMILES TO OTHER PEOPLE

## Introduction

Humour is something that can see us through a range of very difficult and complex situations and also alleviate stress and take the tension out of things when we feel overwhelmed. It is important that bringing smiles to other people is something that we engage in on a regular basis, alongside bringing smiles to our own faces. Humour is different from sarcasm, and needs to be treated carefully in the sense that it can sometimes be easy to use humour to intimidate or tease other people in an inappropriate way. There is a fine line between teasing to engage in humour, and bullying which can cause significant distress to others.

The students are asked to focus upon what it is that makes us laugh and to maintain a laughter log for a weekly period, recording all the times that they found something funny and laughed. They are also asked to think about how they could actually make others feel positive and smile on a regular basis. What is it that they could do to spread the happiness that they might feel for themselves?

### ACTIVITY 1

#### What Makes Us Laugh?

In this activity the students focus on what makes them laugh. What is it that they find humorous in this world? They can think about a range of things here including comedians on the television, magazines, cartoons and special friends who have a predilection for telling jokes. What is important is to focus upon the distinction between unkind laughter and kind laughter. When is it wrong to laugh? Why would it be inappropriate and why do we think we sometimes do laugh at things that are inappropriate to laugh at? For example, someone who falls over or someone who hurts themselves or someone who has a particular physical deformity. What is it about human nature that prompts people to engage in such behaviours and how can we avoid these types of behaviours, particularly when we know them to be negative and to have negative impacts upon others?

### ACTIVITY 2

#### A Laughter Log

In this activity the students are asked to keep a laughter log for a one-week period, recording all the times that they laughed either quietly or out loud. They can then rate the feel-good factor on a scale of 1 to 10 (10 being the best laugh ever). It may also then be useful to consider how each of these situations or laughter-inducing events actually made them feel in the longer term. Did it give them a buzz for the rest of the day? Did it give them a buzz for a few minutes? Is that related to the feel-good factor they've identified on this recording activity sheet.

## ACTIVITY 3

### A Smile a Day...

Some people do say that 'a smile a day keeps the doctor away' just as 'an apple a day keeps the doctor away'! The students are asked to consider why they think this might be the case. Why is smiling important? Who would they smile at, and for what reason? They are asked to record their ideas on the format provided and then to also consider why it might be, at some points in our lives, inappropriate to smile at others. This is particularly important when we think about people who are in vulnerable situations. Do we laugh with them or at them? Which is inappropriate and which is appropriate? This is a useful point of reflection, as being happier in ourselves does not mean that we then have the right to feel any form of contempt for those who are finding it difficult to maintain such a balance in their lives.

## ACTIVITY 4

### Making Others Smile and Feel Happy

Students are finally asked in this session to identify what they can do for others in terms of making them smile and feel happy. What is it that they can do? They are asked to identify key people in their lives, recording their names on the Post-it notes provided and then also recording their ideas as to how they could make them smile and feel happy. They are then asked to spread that happiness and go for it. It will also be interesting to reflect afterwards on feedback from the individuals concerned. Did they notice that the student was making a special effort in order to make them smile and be happy? How important was this to them and is this something that they would welcome in the future in terms of making them feel positive and maintaining their well-being?

## Plenary

Students can finally focus upon the following questions as part of the plenary discussion:

- Why is humour important?
- Can we feel happy all the time?
- What is the difference between laughing at and laughing with someone?
- Is it a useful strategy to try to keep a smiling or happiness diary?
- Does this impact positively on ourselves or others or both?
- Has this session been useful?
- What else could have made the session more helpful? Share ideas.

## What Makes Us Laugh?

This is a thought-storming activity. Think about and identify all the different things that make us laugh and record these on the activity sheet. Then try to distinguish the things that are okay to laugh about and those that may not be.

What makes us laugh?

# HUMOUR: ACTIVITY 2

## A Laughter Log

Take one week! Record all the times that you laughed – either quietly or out loud.

Rate the feel-good factor out of 10 (10 being the best laugh ever!).

|  | Why? | Feel-good factor/10 |
|---|---|---|
| Monday |  |  |
| Tuesday |  |  |
| Wednesday |  |  |
| Thursday |  |  |
| Friday |  |  |
| Saturday |  |  |
| Sunday |  |  |

# HUMOUR: ACTIVITY 3

## A Smile a Day…

Some people say that a smile a day keeps the doctor away! Why do you think this might be the case? Why would you smile? At who? For what reason? At what?

Record your thoughts in the blank smiley faces:

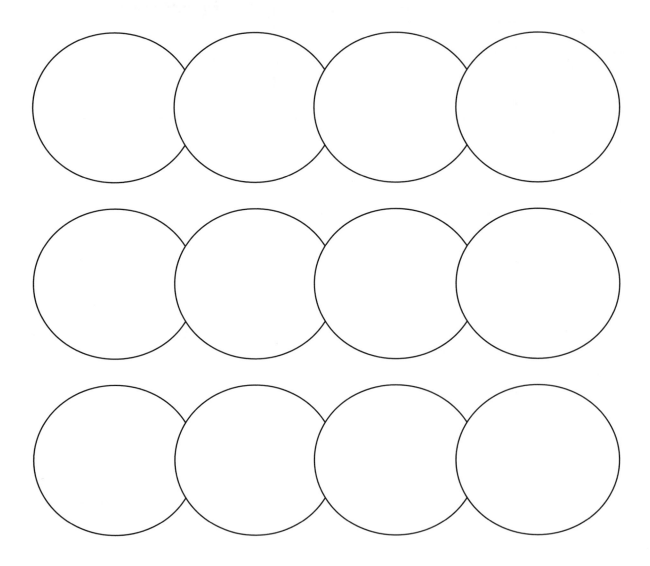

Stop, think and reflect – when would it be wrong to laugh/smile? Under what circumstances/conditions?

# HUMOUR: ACTIVITY 4

## Making Others Smile and Feel Happy

What can you do for others? How can you do this?

Identify key people in your life. Record their names on the Post-it notes and then write down your ideas as to how you can make them smile and feel happy. Then go for it! Spread that happiness!

# Chapter 24

# RELIGIOUSNESS

## HAVING COHERENT BELIEFS ABOUT THE HIGHER PURPOSE OF LIFE

## Introduction

In this chapter the students are introduced to the concept of religiousness and the notion of having a real meaning to our lives and there being some form of higher purpose. It is important for the facilitator, at the outset, not to set up their own views, ideas and belief systems here. They may well have their own notions as to what the higher purpose and meaning of life is but it is important for students to develop their ideas, thoughts, feelings and belief systems in this area. Why are we here? Why are we here now and what is it that we believe? These are epistemological questions that we all need to answer at some point in our lives and there are many psychologists who would put forward the view that having coherent sets of beliefs, and particularly a belief in a higher purpose and meaning of life, can aid our well-being, both in the short and longer term.

The students can also engage in activities focusing upon where they might like to be in the future, what they might want to be and why their goals are deemed to be important both by themselves and others. The notion of Socratic questioning is also introduced when students consider their own beliefs and utilise this process in order to ensure that their core beliefs are clearly stated and articulated.

The final activity requires them to consider their own personal purpose in life. What is it that they think this is? Do they think that there is a higher purpose? Is it religious and is it about doing or being good, and is this process or way of doing good and being good something that gives us the best possible outcome and ensures that we can remain positive in our lives?

### ACTIVITY I

### Why Am I Here? Why Now? What Do I Believe?

These are the big questions that the facilitator can support the students in considering. What is their purpose for being here? Why do they think that they have been created and put upon this earth? Is it to do good? Is it to make a difference? Is it just to live their lives and go through the normal processes that we go through? Do they believe that there is some form of a deity that makes a difference or is controlling their lives? Do they have choice? Are they here to make a good choice and then to proceed to some form of afterlife? It is important that the students can articulate their views independently of the facilitator as these are purely their views and should be valued and respected.

## ACTIVITY 2

### Where Will I Be?

In this activity the students are asked to consider where they will be and what they will be doing at the age of 18 years.

They are asked to work in a group with other students, or alternatively with their facilitator, in order to try and agree on three things that they might all be doing when they are 18. Clearly it is more appropriate for students to work in a smaller group in this activity. They can think about all of these things and identify where they really want to be and also think about why their goals are important. Why, for example, would it be important to have children, to get married, to buy their first car, or have a house or a job? What are their aspirations and why are these important to them and those in their social context?

## ACTIVITY 3

### Socratic Questioning

In this activity the students are asked to work with a partner or their facilitator in order to take turns to engage in the process of Socratic questioning – one acting as the questioner and one acting as the respondent. Step 1 asks them to state a belief, for example: 'I believe that there is a God', 'I believe that all people should have a home', 'I believe that racism is wrong'. In Step 2 the Socratic questioner then asks, 'Why?' This question is posed after every statement made by the first individual. The discussion is continued until the statements become repetitive. This can cause some level of dissonance as what is actually happening here is that a student will be gaining and moving towards their core beliefs. Step 2 can then be worked through making use of other kinds of Socratic questions:

- Is this always the case?
- Can you give me an example of when this is true and when this is not true?
- How can I be sure of what you are saying?
- What would [name someone] say?
- Why is it important?
- How could you look at this another way?
- What evidence do you have?
- What exactly does this mean?

This activity reinforces for students the importance of not only knowing what their belief systems are but also being able to justify them and feeling totally comfortable with them so that they do not induce any kind of dissonance.

## ACTIVITY 4

### Living for a Purpose

In this final activity of this session students are asked to identify their own purpose. What is it that they think their purpose is in this world? What is their higher purpose? Is there one? Is it religious? Is it about being or doing good? Is it about being political or acting in a socially just manner in the world? Is it about changing things that are wrong in the world? Is it about being a good, honest, open and authentic individual? Is it purely about being happy and making others happy or is there a higher deity who has put us on this earth for some other higher purpose?

# Plenary

Students can finally focus upon the following questions as part of the plenary discussion:

- What do we mean by being religious?
- Can we be religious without believing in a god?
- Is it important to have a coherent belief system about the meaning of life and the purpose of life?
- What is our purpose in life?
- Do we share the same purpose?
- Is it important that we share the same purpose?
- Do we believe that people who do have coherent belief systems are happier in this world?
- Is it possible to remain positive, motivated, happy and authentic without such a belief system?
- Has this session been useful?
- What else could have made the session more helpful? Share ideas.

# **RELIGIOUSNESS**: ACTIVITY 1

## Why Am I Here? Why Now? What Do I Believe?

Why am I here?

..........................................................................................................

..........................................................................................................

..........................................................................................................

Why now?

..........................................................................................................

..........................................................................................................

..........................................................................................................

What do I believe?

..........................................................................................................

..........................................................................................................

..........................................................................................................

## The Big Questions! Discuss.

## Where Will I Be?

Where will you be when you are 18?

| | |
|---|---|
| Getting engaged | Getting married |
| Thinking of starting a family | Having a child |
| Finding a part-time job | Thinking of moving out of my parents'/carers' home |
| Moving into my own place with my mates | Taking driving lessons |
| Passing my driving test | Buying my first car |

In your group, can you agree on three things that you would all be doing when you are 18? Is this possible? If so, why? If not, why not?

Think about all these things – where DO you want to be? Why are your goals important?

# **RELIGIOUSNESS**: ACTIVITY 3

## Socratic Questioning

### Step 1

Work with a partner or your facilitator. Each student should take turns to do the following:

1. State a belief, for example 'I believe that there is a God', 'I believe that all people should have a home', 'I believe that racism is wrong'.

2. Challenge the belief, asking the question, 'Why?' Continue the discussion until the statements become repetitive.

### Step 2

Repeat the activity and use other kinds of Socratic questions as follows:

- Is this always the case?

- Can you give me an example of when this is true and when this is not true?

- How can I be sure of what you are saying?

- What would [name] say?

- Why is it important?

- How could you look at this another way?

- What evidence do you have?

- What exactly does this mean?

## Living for a Purpose

What is your purpose? Why do you think this? What is your higher purpose? Is it religious? Is it about being or doing good? Is it political?

List your purposes for being in the box below.

| My purpose for being is to... |
| --- |
| • |
| • |
| • |
| • |
| • |
| • |
| • |
| • |

# FURTHER READING AND USEFUL WEBSITES

The following books and websites contain a wealth of ideas that will be of great value to anyone who is keen to pursue a deeper understanding of a strengths approach and the positive psychology in education.

## Further reading

Altiero, J. (2007) *No More Stinking Thinking: A Workbook for Teaching Children Positive Thinking.* London: Jessica Kingsley Publishers.

Aumann, K. and Hart, A. (2009). *Helping Children with Complex Needs Bounce Back: Resilient Therapy for Parents and Professionals.* London: Jessica Kingsley Publishers.

Brooks, R. and Goldstein, S. (2001) *Raising Resilient Children.* New York: McGraw-Hill. Available at www.drrobertbrooks.com, accessed on 9 December 2011.

Cefai, C. (2008). *Promoting Resilience in the Classroom: A Guide to Developing Students' Emotional and Cognitive Skills.* London: Jessica Kingsley Publishers.

Daniel, B. and Wassell, S. (2002a) *The Early Years: Assessing and Promoting Resilience in Vulnerable Children 1.* London: Jessica Kingsley Publishers.

Daniel, B. and Wassell, S. (2002b) *The Early Years: Assessing and Promoting Resilience in Vulnerable Children 2.* London: Jessica Kingsley Publishers.

Daniel, B. and Wassell, S. (2002c) *The Early Years: Assessing and Promoting Resilience in Vulnerable Children 3.* London: Jessica Kingsley Publishers.

Holt, J. (1967). *How Children Learn.* New York: Pitman Publishing.

McGrath, H. and Noble, T. (2003) *Bounce Back! A Classroom Resiliency Programme.* Harlow: Pearson Longman.

Seligman, M. (1995) *The Optimistic Child.* New York: Houghton Mifflin.

## Web resources

The **Centre for Confidence and Well-being** is based in Glasgow and their website has a whole section on resilience under the Positive Psychology Resources section.
**www.centreforconfidence.co.uk**

**Michael Ungar** is a Professor at the School of Social Work, Dalhousie University, Canada, and is an internationally recognised researcher on the subject of resilience. His website includes information about research projects and has a page for parents.
**www.michaelungar.com**

**Raising Resilient Children**, the website of Robert Brooks and Sam Goldstein, includes information and strategies for teachers and parents. It advertises books and audio materials for sale and has free downloadable information.
**www.raisingresilientkids.com**

**Bounce Back**, the website of Helen McGrath and Toni Noble, includes Positive Practice Frameworks to support individuals and develops resources and strategies for families and schools.
**www.bounceback.com.au**

The **Resiliency Resource Centre** is based in Australia and its website provides information and tips for parents and teachers about how to embrace resilience.
**www.embracethefuture.org.au**

# MENTAL HEALTH FACT SHEET

## What is mental illness?

There is no precise definition as to what constitutes mental illness but it is considered to be a condition that may affect the way we feel and think resulting in an inability to cope with everyday social interactions and routines. Although often considered to be rare, as many as one in four adults may suffer from a form of mental health problems every year and these often begin in childhood. The mental health problems suffered by adolescents in our schools include depression, anxiety, eating disorders, phobias, personality disorders and obsessive compulsive disorders.

## What causes mental illness?

Mental illness is a misleading term as many mental health disorders may have a physical or biological component. For example, those who have a close family member who suffers from depression are more prone to it themselves. Some medications and hormonal changes may also lead to forms of mental illness. Environmental and social factors may include poverty, stress and trauma. Often it is a combination of factors that leads to mental illness.

## What are the signs of mental illness in young people?

In adolescents warning signs may include the following:

- frequent outbursts of anger
- changes in eating habits perhaps leading to considerable weight gain or weight loss
- a prolonged negative mood
- frequently complaining of physical problems, for example headache, stomach ache
- challenges to authority such as theft, truancy and vandalism
- alcohol or drug abuse
- sleeplessness.

## How can I improve my own mental health?

- Avoid substances that are depressants, such as alcohol and tobacco or other drugs.
- Allow yourself plenty of time for a form of relaxation you enjoy. Physical exercise is particularly useful in combating depression.
- Eat a healthy, balanced diet.
- Talk to others about how you are feeling. Hiding your feelings will not make the problem go away and things may build up.
- Set yourself goals and prioritise your challenges.

## How can I get further help?

If you continue to feel depressed or anxious you may need to seek expert help. To do this you should visit your GP, who should be able to help you access the support you need. This might include a referral for counselling, medication such as anti-depressants or a referral to a community mental health team specialist such as a psychiatrist. It is advisable to seek help early to reduce negative outcomes as a result of your illness.

## Referral routes to specialist agencies

### Your GP

Many of the specialist services that are available are accessed through referral by your GP. On diagnosing a mental health issue the GP may prescribe medication such as anti-depressants or tranquilisers. In addition, or as an alternative, a referral may be made to a specialist service.

### Self-referral

Self-referral can be made to self-help groups as appropriate. There are a number of such groups that can offer practical advice and support to individuals. These are very often identified through the websites of national organisations. Local health providers and GPs may also have a list of support that is available in the student's local area.

### Community Mental Health Team

The Community Mental Health Team consists of health and social service professionals working together to provide mental health services. It might include social workers, community psychiatric nurses, psychologists, counsellors, psychiatrists and occupational therapists. Some Community Mental Health Teams will accept self-referrals.

### Hospital

You may be admitted to psychiatric hospital with or without your consent. Compulsory admission to hospital is commonly known as 'being sectioned'. When you are sectioned three people, including a doctor who knows you, must agree that this is necessary.

## Community Psychiatric Nurse

Community Psychiatric Nurses usually visit people in their own homes. They may support people through difficult times and assist with medication.

## Social Services

Social Services can provide services such as home helps, day care services and meals on wheels.

## Occupational Therapists

These will help people adapt to their environment and everyday life. They may use different types of therapy such as art therapy or music therapy. They may also help to rehabilitate people who have been in hospital.

## Counsellors

Counsellors will help people to identify the problems they are facing and discover ways of dealing with them.

## Psychiatrists

Psychiatrists will allocate referrals to other members of the team and will have responsibility for a designated number of patients on a hospital ward. Psychiatrists are able to recommend the involuntary detention of a patient in hospital.

## Self-help groups

There are many local support groups who can offer practical advice and run self-help groups. The next section contains contact details for national organisations that may be able to provide information about local groups and support networks. GPs may also have a list of support that is available in your local area.

## Private counselling/therapy

The United Kingdom Council for Psychotherapy (see contact details in the next section) can provide a list of local psychotherapists. This may, however, be expensive.

# DIRECTORY OF NATIONAL MENTAL HEALTH SERVICES

| Name | What is offered | Contact numbers | Website |
|---|---|---|---|
| AnxietyUK (Formerly National Phobics Society) | Help and support if you have an anxiety condition, information and service to professional health care workers. Members' services including therapy services at reduced rates, members' helpline, bulletin boards and chatrooms. | Tel: 0844 477 5774<br>Fax: 0161 226 7727 | www.anxietyuk.org.uk<br>Email: info@anxietyuk.org.uk |
| Depression Alliance | Publications, national network of local self-help groups. Aims to educate public and raise awareness of depression. | Tel: 020 7633 0557<br>Fax: 020 7633 0559 | www.depressionalliance.org<br>Email: information@depressionalliance.org |
| Manic Depression Fellowship | Self-help groups, information service. Self-management training courses, employment advice, legal advice line, travel insurance scheme. | Tel: 020 7793 2600<br>Fax: 020 7793 2639 | www.mdf.org.uk<br>Email: mdf@mdf.org.uk |
| Mental Health Foundation | Treatments and strategies, how to get help, news events. | Tel: 020 7802 0300<br>Fax: 020 7802 0301 | www.mentalhealth.org.uk<br>Email: mhf@mhf.org.uk |

| MIND (National Association for Mental Health) | Information, advice and support, local MIND network offering supported housing, crisis helplines, drop-in centres, counselling, befriending, advocacy, employment and training schemes. | Tel: 020 8519 2122 Fax: 0208 522 1725 Crisis line: 0845 766 0613 (Mon–Fri 9.15am–5.15pm) | www.mind.org.uk Email: contact@mind.co.uk |
| --- | --- | --- | --- |
| Samaritans | Confidential telephone listening service for lonely people with emotional problems who are despairing and suicidal. Some centres have drop-in facilities. Publications, training courses, teaching resources. | Tel: 0845 790 9090 Fax: 020 7375 2162 Crisis line: 0845 790 9090 (24 hours) | www.samaritans.org Email: jo@samaritans.org |
| Saneline | Out of hours telephone helpline, support during times of crisis, information service, advice on legal rights. | Tel: 020 7375 1002 SANEline: 0845 767 8000 Fax: 020 7375 2162 | www.sane.org.uk Email: sanemail@sane.org.uk |
| United Kingdom Council for Psychotherapy | Publications, information, list of local psychotherapists. | Tel: 020 7014 9955 Fax: 020 7014 9977 | www.psychotherapy.org.uk Email: info@psychotherapy.org.uk |